GUIDEPOSTS FOR THE SPIRIT:

Stories of Courage

Guideposts.
FOR THE
Spirit

STORIES OF
COURAGE

Ideals Publications • Nashville, Tennessee

ISBN 0-8249-4633-2

Published by Ideals Publications
A division of Guideposts
535 Metroplex Drive, Suite 250
Nashville, Tennessee 37211
www.idealsbooks.com

Publisher, Patricia A. Pingry
Associate Publisher, Peggy Schaefer
Permissions Editor, Patsy Jay
Series Designer, Eve DeGrie
Book Designer, Jenny Eber Hancock
Copy Editors, Katie Patton, Melinda Rathjen
Research Assistants, Melinda Rathjen, Julie K. Hogan

Paintings by W. David Ward

Library of Congress Cataloging-in-Publication Data

Guideposts for the spirit : stories of courage.
    p. cm.
  Includes index.
  ISBN 0-8249-4633-2 (alk. paper)
  1. Courage. I. Guideposts (Carmel, N.Y.)
  BJ1533.C8G85 2004
  179'.6—dc22

                                    2004005818

Printed and bound in Italy

10 9 8 7 6 5 4 3 2 1

ACKNOWLEDGMENTS
BARKSDALE, CINDY. "The Decision" from *Mother's Miracles*. Copyright © 1999 by editors Jamie C.
Miller, Laura Lewis, and Jennifer Basye Sander. Published by William Morrow. Used by permission of
HarperCollins Publishers. CHEVALIER, MAURICE. "The Best Advice I Ever Had" from *Chicken Soup for
the Unsinkable Soul*, Health Communications, Inc. Used by permission of the Roger Richman Agency,
Beverly Hills, CA. DRAVECKY, DAVID F. and JANICE. "A Sight That Gives Strength" from *Do Not Lose
Heart*. Copyright © by David and Janice Dravecky III. © 1998 by Thomas Kinkade, Media Arts
Groups, Inc., San Jose, CA. Used by permission of the Zondervan Corporation.
(Acknowledgments continue on page 256.)

CONTENTS

Choosing Faith over Fear

*I will not fear, for you are ever with me,
and you will never leave me to face my perils alone.*
—THOMAS MERTON

FIRESTORM AT OUR BACK DOOR

SHARON DRYDEN

Driving home from the farmers' market in Truckee that hot, windy August afternoon on winding Highway 89 through the Tahoe National Forest, a friend and I were startled to see a tree in flames at a campground along the road. We were in the midst of a dry summer, and any fire in the forest had the potential of becoming dangerous. A U.S. Forest Service worker was standing there with a shovel, looking up at the burning tree. It was not a good sign.

By the time I arrived home a half hour later, my husband, Forest, was running down the driveway, pulling on his volunteer fireman's yellow turnout coat. "There's a fire!" he shouted as he jumped into his pickup.

"I know," I called. "I just saw it."

I watched him disappear down the long residential block on his way to the firehouse, and my stomach fluttered. Although the fire was about fifteen miles away, anything could happen on a day like this.

Suddenly I smelled it. *Smoke!* I craned my neck to see past our white two-story home and the skyscraper pines that framed it. A plume of gray smoke ominously wafted over the mountainside just beyond the golden meadow behind our home. Many ridges sat between the flames and our house, but southwesterly winds were whipping the fire toward us.

As the Loyalton–Sierra Brooks fire engine screamed down the road, an alarm of fear sounded in me as well. I tried to pray away my panic, but it crept into me, like the smoke sneaking over our mountains.

Within hours a smoky, acrid haze pervaded our mile-high valley, so that even home was no longer a haven. Fire trucks streamed in from surrounding counties. News flashes reported that twenty-five-mile-per-hour winds and dry timber were feeding the fire. A numbness washed over me. A firestorm could be raging at our back door in hours.

I hurriedly threw photos and clothing into suitcases, then commandeered our kids—Crystal, fifteen, Matthew, thirteen, and Alayna, seven. They grabbed our two cats, calico Calle and all-black Domino, and our Border collie, Panda. We all jumped into my in-laws' old motor home, stored in our driveway, and in minutes we were headed to my sister Denise's home in Reno, forty miles away. I had to escape; I could not fight another battle.

We had been through so much in the past few years. First, Forest had required surgery for a collapsed lung. Then, our medical insurance company went defunct, nearly bankrupting us. Next, Matthew almost died from leukemia. Exhausted from the financial and emotional toll, I had struggled through anxiety and depression—until we moved into our new home in Sierra Brooks, a rural subdivision four miles north of Loyalton. It was, I felt, a symbol from God: a better life was ahead for us.

In the Sierra we explored streams and mountain paths, discovering flora and wildlife. I loved our dream house, which we had built ourselves—a split-level with vaulted interior ceilings and muted gray-and-pastel furnishings.

But now I feared yet another trial. "It's too much, God," I prayed. "Please make the fire go away."

It didn't. The next morning Forest called to tell me the Cottonwood Fire, as it had been named, was roaring toward our home. "Get our stuff," he said, "the fire's coming." Suddenly I began to quiver. Too shaky to drive, I asked Denise to take me back to our subdivision. When we got there, she had to inch her car around road blockades. Fire trucks guarded every other house, and heat hung in the air.

Three firemen met us at my home and readied it for a fiery battle. They covered windows with blankets, guided our 4-H pig to a trailer, and removed the gas barbecue and woodpile from the fire-facing backyard.

Trying to review my mental lists, I gathered the most important things of our lives. There's money in an envelope, Forest had said. Get Crystal's saddle. Matthew's new air rifle. Alayna's—what did Alayna want? Toys?

The firemen helped me with it all—the computer, photo albums, my wedding dress, Grandma's cookie jar, the children's guardian-angel pictures. My brown Jeep Wagoneer looked like a Dust Bowl migrant family's jalopy stuffed with our most important earthly possessions.

Seeing the panic in my eyes, a friend, Brad, walked up and put his arm around me. A veteran U.S. Forest Service fire manager, he was the commander for the western edge of the fire. "We'll do the best we can, Sharon," he said.

I knew he would: the orange-red firestorm—more than twenty-seven thousand acres in size—was already cresting the western mountainside, threatening his nearby home as well. The heat pushed me in waves; and as I tried to swallow, I tasted soot. I watched the fire hungrily lick its way over the mountain. My heart was pounding. I knew then I was probably seeing my home for the last time.

Back at my sister's home in Reno, exhaustion hit me. Frightened as I was, I hadn't cried yet. I felt I had to hold myself together for the sake of the kids. Grungy and reeking of smoke, I headed for the shower, where my tears fell with the soothing streams.

God, I can't take it anymore. I haven't seen Forest these two days—just two quick calls. Is he okay? And my home may already be gone. Why would you give me a home, a sanctuary, then take it away? I'm so afraid.

I let the water run over me, remembering the last time I had to trust God in a big way. Matthew had been almost four when he had almost died from leukemia. At a nurse's prompting, I sought out the hospital's chapel. There I had prayed, *I love Matthew, Lord, and I want him to live. But he's yours, and I give him back to you.*

It hadn't been an attempt to bargain with God. I had given up my son because I knew God wanted my surrender and trust most of all. And soon Matthew was on the road to healing and complete remission.

Now I prayed in the shower, *Lord, you have faithfully brought us through each hardship. Why should you not be trustworthy again?*

I sighed. I would still trust God for everything in my life. There would be no trying to bargain. As the water soothed my aching body, he calmed my soul. I knew then that no matter what the outcome of the Cottonwood Fire, God would take care of all of us.

Just minutes after my shower my husband's sister telephoned. "The fire's on the six o'clock news, Sharon. Go watch it."

Grimly I sat on the couch. The kids were still outside playing. Denise was at the grocery store. Trying to hold back tears, I rested my face in my hands and watched the TV. A white-haired reporter in a yellow firefighter's shirt was reporting live. My neighborhood stood in the background; smoke billowed through the pines on the hills behind the houses.

Then suddenly the scene changed and I saw it. Our home! The front of the house filled the television screen. I held my breath as the shots changed every few seconds . . . the firestorm rushing toward our house . . . flames swallowing hundred-foot trees in a moment . . . Brad lighting a backfire at the edge of our yard . . . one of our trees bursting into flames, just feet from the house . . . a fireman spraying foam over the kids' swing set . . . a helicopter dropping water from a bucket.

What happened then so shocked me that I wasn't sure I was seeing what I thought I saw. A sudden force of wind blew back the massive wall of flames—and in an instant the firestorm switched its course! Instead of heading toward our home, it turned almost completely around and rushed south. I gasped as the reporter confirmed that the fire had not damaged a single house. "Oh, thank you, God . . . thank you!" I almost shouted.

It was several days until things returned to normal. Another arm of the fire continued to threaten nearby Loyalton for two days. The population tripled in size during that week, as more than twenty-five hundred firefighters from the Forest Service and California Department of Forestry and volunteers from all over the West converged on our town of twelve hundred. Schools, the city park, and surrounding alfalfa fields looked like war encampments.

Finally, the fire burned itself out near the Nevada border north of Reno. More than 48,600 acres of Tahoe National Forest and grazing land were consumed by the Cottonwood Fire of 1994. But not a home was lost—not a life. Some say the backfire helped switch the fire's direction, saving the houses. But even the fire manager in charge, Brad, said it was a miracle.

The next afternoon I returned home alone. As I pulled into the driveway, I noticed a television-news team interviewing a group of firefighters. I timidly approached, and gasped when I saw Forest standing with them. I had almost not recognized him. He was covered with soot, his thick brown hair was rumpled and exhaustion was etched into his face. And his boots! The soles had been melted away! The intensity of the danger hit me, and I fell into his arms.

News reporters moved toward us. One newswoman—twentyish, dressed in jeans, perky in the midst of us battle-weary locals—brushed aside her layered brown hair. "Ma'am," she said, "I bet you feel really lucky." She smiled sympathetically as she poised her pencil over her notepad.

I looked at her in disbelief. As the news camera zoomed in, I shook my head and measured my words. "Lucky," I said, "is finding a penny. This has nothing to do with luck."

And as I walked back to our home with my arm around my husband and his around me, I thanked God. For he had shown me once again that when I put my faith completely in him, he takes care of my needs more wonderfully than I can even ask. He is worthy of my trust—every time.

*Faith in yourself and faith in God are the
keys to the mastery of fear.*
—HAROLD SHERMAN

LOOK OUT, FEAR, HERE COMES FAITH

MARION BOND WEST

A forced myself to remain calm so I wouldn't lose control of the car. "Pray, Jeremy, pray!" I cried out to my fourteen-year-old son sitting in the back seat. In one split second, an afternoon outing to a football game had turned into the most horrible nightmare imaginable: my husband, in the seat beside me, appeared to be dying.

Jerry had come home from work early so he could see Jon, one of our twin sons, play in the first football game of the season. It was rare for Jerry to be home early. I was delighted to be able to be with him. I'd just as soon we weren't going to a football game, but it was a sunny Thursday in September and I was happy. Carefree. I felt sort of a hint of apprehension when Jerry first came home. He said that he felt odd. He never complained and was never sick. *He's probably just a little tired,* I reasoned. But when we left the house to pick up Jeremy at school, Jerry said, "Why don't you drive?"

I brushed away his strange comment. But as I drove, for some reason I didn't understand, I kept looking at him. Something about him seemed different. I couldn't put my finger on it. Then, as we waited in the car in front of the school for Jeremy to come out, I asked Jerry to roll down his window. "It's hot," I said. I watched in total disbelief as my husband tried over and over to figure out how to roll down the car window. He touched many different things in the car. He even leaned over the back seat. *Dear Lord, what are we in for?* I thought. Jerry and I stared at each other in amazement.

Jeremy came out from school, jumped in the backseat, and I drove away. "Do you want me to head for the doctor's?" I asked Jerry, forcing my voice to remain calm. But even then I knew there wasn't time. Something monstrous was bearing down on us and it was coming fast. I didn't know what "it" was, only that it was imminent and that we desperately needed protection.

"It's not my heart," Jerry said, looking stunned. "My normal blood pressure is one-twenty over eighty. I've just had a physical." But his eyes didn't look right. They were too set. He didn't seem to hear me. As I drove, trying to figure out what to do, Jerry suddenly fell against me hard. Unconscious. His coloring was bluish; he was having trouble breathing.

"Jerry!" I screamed. At the same moment I caught a glimpse of Jeremy's face in the rearview mirror. It was crumpled like tissue paper. "Daddy, Daddy," he shouted. His face reflected my own feelings. The car seemed to fill up with Fear, overpowering Fear, just as if we'd suddenly plunged into a river and were filling up with water. Our only small "air pocket" of hope was prayer. "Pray," I said to Jeremy again. "Pray, pray!" He dropped his head and his lips began to move. I prayed aloud, eyes wide open, as I drove with one hand and held Jerry up with the other. I could not let him fall to the floor. If he fell, my faith would topple too. He was very heavy, but I held him erect. Was my husband going to die sitting beside me on a sunny afternoon? Was our life together over so quickly?

All this took place in a matter of seconds. Then something I'd read the day before forced its way into my confused mind; in the Bible we are told eighty times to "fear not." I made a decision not based on feelings. No matter how difficult, I would "fear not." Then and there, I chose Faith over Fear. Again joining Jeremy in prayer, I said aloud, "Dear Jesus, help us. We need you. I trust you. Jesus, Jesus, Jesus . . ."

Immediately a plan came into my mind. *Keep driving. Very fast. You can do it. I'm going ahead of you. Blow the horn. Keep praying.* I didn't dare look down to see how fast we were going. I didn't even glance at Jerry. I knew where we were headed now—to a nearby ambulance stand. I could see it clearly in my mind. My faith began to grow as my arm on Jerry's chest suddenly touched the area of his heart. There was a strong, steady beat. *Thank you, Jesus.* Faith, like a scrawny plant, stood erect and bloomed. I kept praying.

Scriptures on faith, a topic Jerry and I had been studying in a new Sunday school class, began coming to me as if on a ticker tape. *What time I am afraid, I will trust in thee. God hath not given us the spirit of fear; but of power, and of love, and of a sound mind. Be strong, fear not: behold, your God will come. Fear not: for I am with thee. Be not afraid, only believe. There is no fear in love; but perfect love casteth out fear. God is our refuge and strength. Therefore will not we fear. Fear ye not, stand still, and see the salvation of the Lord.*

The ambulance attendants had heard my horn blowing from quite a distance. They were outside waiting for us. Almost before I stopped the car, Jerry was being lifted out and placed on a stretcher. I picked up Jerry's glasses from the car's floorboard and answered the attendant's rapid-fire questions, not sure all the while if Jerry was just unconscious or dead. Yet a great sense of calm seemed to cover me. Looking at him I thought: *You can't be dead. No one simply dies wearing blue jeans and a shirt that says "Adidas" on a beautiful afternoon in September.* Just then one of the ambulance attendants said that he had a good pulse.

Faith and I rejoiced. Fear skulked away. I knew Fear would return. We piled into the ambulance and headed for the nearest hospital. In the emergency room, as people worked with Jerry, he came to and asked, "Did we miss the game?" For him that was a very normal response.

"We'll make the next one," I said. I wanted to add that I'd never complain about not liking football again, but there wasn't time. Whatever had happened to him was happening again.

Fear taunted me: "He's not all right." Was he slipping into unconsciousness? "See how bad he looks."

What time I am afraid, I will trust in thee.

The doctor took me into a room and explained that Jerry would need all kinds of complicated tests. I made the decision to transfer him to another hospital where the needed equipment was available. The doctor looked me right in the eyes and said, "Something has triggered two seizures in your husband. We are probably dealing with a brain tumor or a stroke. You need a neurologist, maybe a neurosurgeon." I heard his words, but somehow the words "brain tumor" and "stroke" whizzed by me, like badly thrown footballs. I didn't reach out for them. . . . those words couldn't be for us.

"Brain tumor," Fear screamed at me.

What time I am afraid, I will trust in thee.

Then we were in the ambulance again, speeding to another hospital. Friends had arrived and taken Jeremy with them. Our older daughter Julie had come to the hospital and now rode with us on our second ambulance ride. I happened to glance in my purse and see Jerry's billfold and glasses. They looked out of place. "Your husband's not a well man. You have to take over," Fear chanted.

What time I am afraid, I will trust in thee.

We met the neurologist, a woman whom Jerry and I both liked immediately. She asked us all kinds of questions. We answered each one. Jerry touched his nose countless times at her command and began right away to undergo tests on a "stat" basis. A spinal tap was first. The doctor spoke of a possible stroke. We got word that the CAT scan was normal. No sign of a brain tumor! Jerry winked at me. Faith was winning this round. As Jerry was being admitted to intensive care, he only asked one question: "Mannie, did we win the ball game?"

I had anticipated the question, made a quick phone call, and had the answer. "Yep. Twenty-seven to seven. Our favor. Jon made several good plays."

He smiled happily. It was just as well I didn't know that his condition for the next few days would be listed as critical. I made the difficult decision to go home and sleep and be with the children. On my way home Fear insisted that I should have stayed. "What if . . . ?" Fear suggested.

What time I am afraid, I will trust in thee.

I woke up several times during the night. Fear hung heavy in my room and tried to tell me that all was not well with Jerry. I got up and read the 91st Psalm and went to sleep thinking, *I will not be afraid of the terror by night. . . .*

The morning brought unspeakable joy—seeing Jerry. I arrived at the hospital just as the sun was coming up. Jerry seemed in good spirits, but very groggy from sedation. We were overjoyed that he was transferred to a private room.

As the days passed, we had long talks. Jerry spoke openly of his love for me, looking right into my eyes. I, being a hopeless romantic, loved it. I knew he loved me in his own quiet way. But what joy to be told daily. I felt rather like a teenager in love for the first time. Rather than concentrate on his illness or any problems, I found myself constantly thinking how much I loved him. It was so much more than I had thought I loved him. "We are really one now," Jerry said one day as I held his hand. I loved spending ten or twelve hours a day with him. We even had our own little revival on Sunday morning in his room.

I had brought some inspirational tapes. Jerry isn't much of a tape man but he agreed to listen to one. He had on new red pajamas and looked good. The doctor was still doing a lot of tests and hadn't told us much. The results of some of the blood tests were not what the doctor wanted. And Jerry ran a fever from time to time. But Fear was not in the room that morning. The minister on the tape asked, "What do you need Jesus to do for you right now, by faith?" And then, in an emotion-filled voice, the minister sang, "No one ever cared for me like Jesus . . . I would tell you how he changed my life completely . . . But I'll never know just why he came to save me. . . ."

I knew something marvelous and powerful was about to happen. It was coming from the Source of Faith. I found myself remembering a day ten years before when in my utter desperation I had surrendered myself and my life to Jesus Christ. Like most people, I had come to him before in bits and pieces, afraid to commit myself totally. But one day I did it. I said to Jesus, "Here's all of me." I shed tears of joy. And my life was never the same again.

Jerry was crying now, softly, joyfully. I didn't have to ask my questions. I understood. I watched as Faith embraced Jerry and transformed him. "He can have me . . . all of me," Jerry said simply.

After that experience, we didn't expect to hear from Fear anymore. We should have known better. The very next day, late in the afternoon, Fear came disguised as depression. I saw it the minute it touched Jerry. The sparkle left his blue eyes. His shoulders sagged. He stared out the window, not speaking. He was grim. "Please don't be sad. Don't let depression get you down," I said. "We have to stay above that." I knew he was thinking about the future. There were so many unanswered questions. I couldn't seem to reach him. Fear moved about the room freely now. "Jerry, we have to praise God. The Bible says to praise in all situations, whether we feel like it or not." We both knew the principle well, but doing it was something else. His sadness was reaching me too. Fear couldn't win now. Faith was far out in front.

"Let's sing, Jer." I was near tears for the first time since this whole thing started. There was no response from my husband.

"Jerry, please. Look at me."

Nothing.

Fear closed in for the kill. I couldn't see Jerry too well through my tears.

"Jer, would you whistle?" My husband sings off-key sometimes, but he can whistle beautifully. Lots of times he just starts whistling a tune and I guess the name of it. It is sort of an old game we've played since we were dating.

"Please, Jerry. For me."

He turned and looked at me and saw my tears. His eyes said clearly that he didn't want to whistle. But then the first sweet, clear notes penetrated the room. I spoke the words to the now familiar tune. "No one ever cared for me like Jesus. . . ."

Jerry sat up in bed, the sparkle back in his eyes. He smiled at me and kept whistling. I smiled back and sang the words softly. Fear cowered somewhere in a corner. Faith stalked the room like a giant.

Late the next afternoon, just as the last rays of sunlight shone through the window, we were both silent for a long time. It was a good silence. I felt we were thinking the same thoughts, and I loved that. Jerry broke the silence. He looked at me, positively beaming as I sat on his bed. He said with certainty, "I'm all right now. I'm all right."

"Yes! That's exactly what I was thinking." I laid my head on his chest and we held on to each other. I had the distinct impression that the unseen arms of Faith held both of us like rescued children.

Jerry was released from the hospital on a beautiful, sunny morning, with word from the neurologist that he most certainly could attend Jon's game that day.

Our next test of faith came that very afternoon. Once again we were picking up

Jeremy from school and planned to go to Jon's football game. It was Thursday, three o'clock, exactly like one week before. We sat in front of the school. Without thinking, I said, "Will you roll down the window, Jer? It's hot."

Then I remembered. The whole scene tried to flash before me. Jerry didn't respond for a split second. Fear was waiting for any opportunity to attack. Fear lunged into the car and insisted, "It's about to happen again!"

Then Jerry, laughing at my apprehension, rolled down the window and winked at me. I laughed, too. A gentle breeze blew in through the open window, bringing with it sweet Faith. Jerry reached over and held my hand.

We know there will be more medical tests, and I suspect our faith will be tested again and again. Meanwhile, life goes on as normal—no, much better than normal. When a husband and wife fall in love all over again, after being married almost twenty-five years, nothing is ever normal again.

Whatever other tests we have to face, we'll face them head-on. We've already gotten through the toughest one. We have looked Fear right in the face and said, "Look out, Fear, here comes Faith!"

Fear knocked at the door. Faith answered.
And lo, no one was there.

—AUTHOR UNKNOWN

SOLO FLIGHT

PAUL LASSALLE

My family and I carefully unfurled the bright red-and-white nylon fabric of my hot-air balloon, *Rising Spirit*. The lazy light of a summer dawn broke softly across the dew-soaked field just outside Picayune, Mississippi. It was July 14, 1992, and the sharp wake-up calls of the birds rode the Gulf Coast breeze.

Soon I would be riding aloft on the winds, floating above the earth in a basket suspended beneath the balloon. There was excitement as we worked.

This was the moment I had trained and studied for, my first solo flight in a hot-air balloon. My instructor, Mike, was there, as was Becky, my wife; our twenty-five-year-old son, Steven; my father-in-law, Jack; and my niece Tracie. They would be my ground crew, helping to inflate *Rising Spirit*, then following me on the ground in a chase vehicle once I became airborne. Airborne is the perfect term to describe what happens to a balloon in flight, for you are literally borne by the wind. Ideal ballooning weather is clear, dry, and not too hot, with winds no greater than eight knots. Gustier than that and we don't take off. More than in any other type of flying, a balloon is dependent on the wind to determine its flight path and speed. Altitude is controlled by heating or cooling the air in the fabric envelope with the burner. When it comes time to land, the pilot releases air from the balloon by pulling a cord attached to a vent at the top of the envelope. Landing is the trickiest part of flying a balloon. I had made a few supervised landings with Mike in the basket with me, but this time I was on my own.

We began to inflate *Rising Spirit* by blowing air into the huge fabric envelope with a powerful fan. I then heated the air in the envelope with one of two propane burners, causing the balloon to slowly stand upright. Becky and I had bought the red-and-white beauty two months earlier because we wanted to get into an exciting hobby. I had always dreamed of flying, and ballooning seemed to be a pure and natural way of doing it.

I've been described as a take-control kind of man. As a captain for the New Orleans Fire Department, I had commanded companies of firefighters and had taken responsibility for decisions that often put me and my men in harm's way. Being a contractor also, I enjoy supervising a job. If you're going to do something, you might as well be in charge of it. Maybe that's why ballooning was so alluring to me. Piloting took skill and decisiveness, but at the same time I was at the mercy of the wind. It was a challenge and an adventure.

Stepping into the basket, I felt butterflies in my stomach. Above me billowed *Rising Spirit*, nearly seven stories tall. Becky was preserving the scene on video for the Lassalle family archives. "Have a good one," she shouted, waving with her free hand. "Look out for power lines!" Statistically, ballooning is safer than driving the family car, but one thing pilots have to be on the watch for are high-voltage wires, which can turn a balloon into a torch in seconds.

Becky jumped into our van, Steven at the wheel and Mike and the others in back. "See ya in about an hour," I shouted. I fired up the burner and *Rising Spirit* lifted off.

The ground quickly slipped away, and somewhere below I heard a dog's fading bark. I thought of Psalm 104: *Bless the Lord . . . who stretchest out the heavens like a curtain . . . who maketh the clouds his chariot: who walketh upon the wings of the wind . . .*

I had lived much of my life without faith. I had been raised in a good home but my religion had fallen away from me like the ground below did now. By my teens I was dodging church to spend Sundays doing my own thing. Even after I married, I used to stay home tinkering in the garage while Becky and the kids went to services.

A sudden bump, as if *Rising Spirit* had hit a pothole in the sky, snapped me back to reality. I clutched the sides of the basket and looked up into the mouth of the balloon, half expecting to see a fatal tear in the fabric above me, but the nylon was smooth and taut. What could have caused the disturbance? My mind raced for an explanation. *You should have been paying more attention*, I scolded myself. Suddenly I noticed the treetops rising to meet me. I fired both burners to gain altitude. Nothing. The pilot lights were out! I grabbed my electric lighter and reignited them. The burners sputtered, then fired, and the balloon gently rose again. At one thousand feet I breathed a long sigh of relief. I was out of danger.

That was about as much excitement as I wanted for this flight. But the crisis reminded me of just how little control I had up here alone in the sky. *In a way*, I thought, *it's a little like the struggle I have with faith.* I had begun my journey back to faith when my daughter, Susan, then a young girl, asked me why I didn't attend church with the rest of the family. The question shamed and alarmed me. Then, a little while later, when my men and I were fighting a house fire, we were unable to rescue one of the residents. That death left me searching for meaning in my own life; and through a series of events, I was drawn back to church and the Bible, comforted by the belief that someone much greater than myself was in control. Becky and I recommitted ourselves to a marriage based on spiritual principles. But I still had trouble relinquishing charge to God. God could be the copilot, but I still yearned to be the pilot.

As I drifted, life below seemed so distant, soundless, and ordered. I was struck by the peacefulness of the sky, so peaceful that time seemed to freeze. When I checked my watch, I realized that I had been aloft for nearly forty-five minutes. Time to find a flat place to land.

I spotted a nearby hayfield and pulled the vent control line, but I miscalculated the distance of a fence and had to fire the burners quickly to avoid a collision. My face reddened with self-annoyance. What would Mike think? I spotted a second field. "Don't blow it," I muttered as I again began easing *Rising Spirit* down for a landing. Then, at the last second, I saw them: a criss-crossing of power lines glinting menacingly in the morning sun.

The lines seemed to be rushing straight toward me. I could be electrocuted if I came in contact with them. Gritting my teeth, I turned the burners on full blast. Unlike a plane or hang glider, a balloon doesn't respond immediately to a command; it takes a little time for the air to heat. The lines came closer. I held my breath. At the last moment *Rising Spirit* swooped above the danger.

The field swept into the distance behind me. *This isn't as easy as I thought.* Suddenly I felt panicky, out of control. I looked for another place to land, but all I saw was miles and miles of thick woods. I checked my fuel supply: about a half of one tank remaining. When it ran out *Rising Spirit* would come down, trees or no trees.

The balloon was picking up speed quickly. Ten knots, fifteen—far too fast for a safe landing. The only thing to do was hit the burners and try to find a higher altitude where the wind was blowing in another direction. Yet that would use up more fuel.

I was truly frightened. Feeling powerless, I raised my eyes and cried out, "Help me. Take control of this situation. Lord, find me a safe place to land!" With that prayer, a feeling of calm came over me. My fingers unclenched and my body wavered with relief. I felt like a tub when the drain plug has been pulled, the fear swirling away like dirty bathwater.

The rushing wind roared in my ears and the landscape below sped by. I had no idea where Becky and the crew were. They must have lost sight of me by now. All at once the trees opened up, and a small clearing appeared directly ahead of me. I had to act fast. I jerked on the cooling vent and *Rising Spirit* dropped. Five hundred feet. Three hundred. The clearing was a small pasture with horses and cows. I would have to be careful not to cause a stampede. Two hundred feet. Suddenly I saw them, two of the biggest bulls I had ever seen. And me coming down in a big red balloon!

Lord, I trusted you to find me a safe place to land, and I trust you completely with those bulls.

I held on tight as the basket smacked into the ground, shot up, and pounded the earth again. The horses just stared and the cows walked casually to the side of the pasture as I bounced along. The basket tipped and I clutched the sides more tightly as the wind pulled the balloon like a child pulling a toy, dragging the basket another 150 feet.

Finally *Rising Spirit* lurched to a halt. When my head stopped spinning, I looked around. Behind me, maybe fifty yards off, stood the bulls, contentedly munching grass. Running across the field toward me were Steven and Mike, trailed by a surprised farmhand. They had stayed with me all the way.

"Daddy, that was some ride!" Steven exclaimed as he and the other men approached me.

"You got caught in some nasty wind shear," added Mike. "It's a miracle you kept control."

I smiled at Mike's innocent comment. *No, it's a miracle I gave up control,* I thought. My first solo flight had been a success. But I had just been along for the ride.

Fear is faith that it won't work out.
—Sister Mary Tricky

The Ocala Ordeal

Carol L. Best

t was after eleven o'clock the night of January 28, 1995, when Roland and I finally reached the dirt road leading to the campgrounds in the Ocala National Forest. Our two grandchildren, Eric and Joel, ages three and six, had been missing in the dense forest since ten that morning. A rescue center had been set up on the campgrounds by the sheriff's department, and there we found my son and his wife, frightened and exhausted.

Michele rushed to us, her voice choked with tears. "Tim and I were cleaning rooms for the Elderhostel," she sobbed, "and the boys were right outside collecting moss for a school science project. Not five minutes later, they were gone. It was like the forest just swallowed them up."

"We'll find them," I told her. "Don't lose faith."

Not being allowed to venture into the woods, we stayed near the rescue center in a camper trailer. Tim, Michele, Roland, and I prayed into the wee hours of the morning. Finally I walked outside to stare at the black wall of trees. An occasional rustle of leaves or burst of birdcall would send my mind spinning, imagining my grandchildren huddled somewhere out there in the darkness—towheaded Joel, the big-brother protector, and brown-eyed, quiet Eric, cold and afraid, both of them curled up under the brush together to keep warm.

How could I convince Tim and Michele to trust their children to God's care if I wasn't sure how they would survive that forest all alone? My mind went back thirty years, to when I watched Tim's two younger brothers succumb to hyaline membrane disease. The vicious pain of that loss returned to me. I knew exactly the helplessness my son and daughter-in-law were feeling. Was I strong enough to help them through this?

The black forest wall stood before me like a prop from a fairy tale. I recalled the image that had come to me as we drove through the rain to get here, of Eric and Joel walking hand in hand on a path. *They will be okay*, I'd thought. I wanted to hold on to that image, that hope. *God, send angels to watch over them and keep them safe*, I asked now.

Sheriff Knupp came from the rescue center before dawn to update us. "We're sorry we couldn't search more in the night, but within the hour we'll be sending out Humvees, horses, volunteers, and dogs."

"What do you think our chances are?" asked Roland.

"Well, we know the older boy had wrapped candy and the little fella was in diapers. We feel certain the dogs will be able to locate those items soon."

"The boys don't have any jackets on," said Michele, her face flushed from crying.

"It's been a warm night," the sheriff offered. "Hopefully, we'll come across those candy wrappers or the diaper. Your sons can't just disappear into thin air."

When dawn finally came that Sunday, the search team assembled. Military crews arrived, as well as hundreds of volunteers. At one point, a three-mile line of cars and trucks inched bumper-to-bumper along the dirt road. I saw housewives, farmers, nurses, paramedics, business people, a pregnant woman, and men and women of every age. Were these the angels I had prayed for?

The sheriff organized people into groups and briefed them. Walking arm's length from one another, they were to look for footprints while calling out the boys' names. Again and again these human angels went back to search deeper and deeper in the damp, mucky, vine-entangled woods, and each time I prayed for their safety.

Throughout that long second day, people in the camp brought us blankets and food; many reached out to hug us or pray with us. At the same time, the FBI was putting Michele and Tim through a long, torturous interrogation. As parents, they were suspects in the boys' disappearance. Michele was subjected to a lie-detector test, which she failed when the agent asked, "Do you know where your boys are?"

"It was my responsibility," she cried. "I should have known!" It was hard to comfort her.

There had been no trace of the boys all day—no candy wrappers, no diapers, no footprints. That night Tim came outside and sat down beside me on the grass.

"Haven't slept yet," I said, "have you?"

His bottom lip quivered. "Mom, Michele and I think our boys are dead. We don't think we'll ever see them again," he said.

I put my arm around his shoulder and held him close. "Don't say that, Tim."

"I believe it's true," he said, "and what's worse is that they think Michele and I are to blame."

Gently I rubbed his back. "If we close the door to faith, God can't do his job. He can work with us only as our faith will allow."

"We can't go on without Joel and Eric, Mom," he cried. "What are we going to do?"

I held Tim and watched the moths circling the lamps. "God knows our needs, and I know he will be with our boys," I told Tim. "He'll keep you strong and give you the courage to get through this, if you'll let him."

Monday dawned with weather reports of rain and freezing temperatures. I couldn't let myself think of the approaching cold or give up my vision of the two boys walking along a path. Meanwhile I watched rescue workers search Deerhaven Lake, not far from the campgrounds. Helicopters lifted to search and set down again with nothing. I struggled within myself. Were my faith and hope only a fairy tale?

The day wore on, the third of our ordeal. A sad quiet seemed to blanket everyone and everything. Tim and I walked along the edge of the moss-covered trees and rocks, where Joel and Eric must have gone days before. The sky clouded over. A cool breeze began to push at the trees, turning their leaves pale, a sign of rain here in Florida. I slipped my arm around Tim's waist for comfort. Again I tried to envision the boys on the path.

As we returned to camp, we heard a man shouting happily from the rescue center. People were cheering. "They found them!" someone yelled. "They found the boys!" Michele ran up and leaped into Tim's arms, and he spun her in circles while the entire crowd clapped for joy.

"One of our searchers heard a faint cry," Sheriff Knupp explained, "and the man pushed through a patch of saw-toothed palmettos to find the boys standing there, holding hands. Joel said in a hoarse voice, 'Please take us back to the campgrounds to where our mommy and daddy are.'"

"Where were they?" I asked. "Are they okay?"

"The little rascals got more than two miles away, behind Deerhaven Lake," he said. "They're mosquito-bit and a little dehydrated and hungry, but they seem to be okay."

The boys were carried first by horseback, then by truck, to camp, where they rushed into the waiting arms of Tim and Michele. The candy wrappers were tucked in Joel's pocket. "My mommy told me not to litter," he said. The diaper had been buried for the same reason. "And we didn't drink out of the dirty lake or eat any bad berries," Joel said.

"Were you real scared at night?" I asked.

"No, Gramma. When it got dark, we curled up together and went to sleep, and when it got light, we tried to call out to the helicopters to come and find us."

Joel and Eric were the center of a statewide television broadcast, during which our family thanked the earthly angels who came to our rescue. On live TV, I watched Joel reach out to rub the back of Eric's neck while he spoke very plainly. "I was the onliest one to rescue both of our lives," he said. "He's my brother and I love him."

In [Christ] we have boldness and access with confidence by the faith of him.
—EPHESIANS 3:12

IN PERFECT HARMONY

NAOMI JUDD

Once liver disease forced me to retire from my country music career in 1991, I thought people wouldn't be interested in my life anymore. Turns out they have more questions than ever. Folks always ask: How did a girl from sleepy little Ashland, Kentucky, who'd never sung a note in public, end up performing concerts all across America? How did a single mom who just wanted to find steady work become a country music star? How did I keep from losing my spirit when I lost the career I loved? How did I find healing from a devastating chronic illness?

The answers are really different verses of the same song—the song of faith, of believing, of seeing not with the eyes, but with the mind and heart and soul.

The first verse came to me in the spring of 1975, after I'd moved back to Kentucky with my daughters, Wynonna, ten, and Ashley, six. I needed to put the troubles of the last six years in Los Angeles behind me—a divorce from the girls' dad (whose job had taken us to California), a string of dead-end jobs (all I could get without a college degree), a stint on welfare. I wanted to give my girls the stable upbringing they deserved. Where better to do that than in the Kentucky hills where my roots were?

We stayed in a dirt-cheap rental cabin near Berea while I started my nursing school classes. I promised Wy and Ashley, "This is just until we find a place of our own." Except six months later we were still there.

Had I uprooted my girls for nothing? One day in May when they were at school, I turned on the radio, opened the window, and sat down on a blanket right outside so I could listen to music while I studied. The Stanley Brothers' achingly beautiful bluegrass tunes came on. I closed my eyes and drifted back to my childhood, back to the days when God was as real as our house at 2237 Montgomery Avenue. *Lord, even if I can't lay eyes on you, I still know you're real,* I prayed. *So I'm going to believe the same with this home we're searching for. I will hold on to this image in my heart—a cozy little house in the hills—and have faith that you'll lead us to it.*

The following evening the girls and I were driving through Berea when we saw an elderly woman slip and fall. We stopped to check on her. She'd twisted her ankle badly, and the aspiring nurse in me insisted we take her to the emergency room. We got to talking, and I confided my difficulty in finding a home.

The next day I found a note in my mailbox at nursing school from Margaret Allen, a friend of the woman we'd stopped to help. Mrs. Allen had a house she wanted to show me.

Her directions took us to the tiny town of Morrill. We turned off Big Hill Road and at the crest of a knoll stood a two-story house with a big front porch and apple trees dotting the yard. An elderly lady stepped out and introduced herself as Margaret Allen. "Welcome to Chanticleer," she said. "Your new home."

I was speechless. "It's completely furnished, linens, dishes, silverware, everything. . . . " she said. "Come, I'll show you."

Inside, the house was even lovelier, like something out of a fairy tale, filled with antiques. "Mrs. Allen, we couldn't possibly afford to rent this place!" I gasped.

"Could you afford one hundred dollars a month?" she asked. "I don't need the money, just the right people to have it."

We moved into Chanticleer in June, and it was there on that big front porch we discovered something that would change our lives. Someone had given me an old guitar, and just for fun I brought it out. Wynonna took to the guitar like a bee to honeysuckle, returning to it again and again.

I bought Wy her own guitar, a used but nice instrument. I unearthed an old bluegrass album by Hazel and Alice in the used bin at a record store. Two women singing, their voices blending in a way that sent shivers up our spines. That was the sound of our Kentucky hills! Wy and I taught ourselves every song on that record. Strange thing was, I'd never sung before, not even in church—I'd felt too shy to do more than mouth the hymns. But on the porch with Wynonna, a voice I never knew I had came out, harmonizing naturally with hers, a musical expression of our family bond. The first song we learned all the way through was "A Mother's Smile."

It wasn't till four years later that I learned the second verse of my own song of faith. By then I knew music was Wy's gift, her destiny. My job was to go with her and make sure it didn't become her downfall too. I'd started writing songs for us to sing together, and we moved to Nashville—Music City, USA—on the condition that she finish high school. I house-sat while we looked for a place in the country-side to rent. I had to wait for my Tennessee nursing certification to come in, so I took a low-paying job as an assistant to a booking agent on Music Row.

One Friday night that summer of 1979, Larry Strickland, an amazing bass singer whose band my boss managed, asked me out. Since I didn't go to bars or clubs, I suggested we check out an old property I'd heard about in Franklin, just out-side Nashville. We stood in the moonlight looking at the neglected house and just talked. Then he kissed me softly and that was it. I was head over heels.

Sunday after church I called Larry on the road only to find he was out with another woman. My heart broke. That night the person I was house-sitting for told me he would be returning soon, and we'd have to move on. I felt so defeated. No partner, no real job, no place to call home. Had I dragged us right back into the mess I'd worked so hard to get us away from?

That's when I remembered a verse from Hebrews I'd heard in church that morning: "Now faith is the substance of things hoped for, the evidence of things not seen." *God, I'm going to believe that all the dreams I have in my heart are as real as you are,* I prayed. Our own home, with everything in it working. A car that didn't clank, smoke or break down. A job that would leave me enough to buy my daughters Christmas presents. And finally, the wildest dream of all, a career in country music.

I pictured the future I hoped for. I formed a clear image of it in my mind. Then I set about making it happen. I stepped out in faith and rented the run-down house in Franklin for three hundred and fifty dollars a month. The girls and I fixed it up, one thing at a time. And with a lot of talking and praying, Larry and I patched things up too.

My nursing certification came in that winter. I signed up with a nurses' registry so I would have flexibility in my work schedule to check out music-related opportunities, like sweet-talking a local TV producer into letting Wynonna and me perform on the early morning *Ralph Emery Show* on February 11, 1980. We became regulars on the show. One of my patients, a teenager recovering from a car accident, recognized me from TV. She introduced me to her dad, record producer Brent Maher. I mustered up the nerve to give him a demo tape Wynonna and I had made on our Kmart tape recorder. Right away Brent understood our unique sound. He and manager Ken Stilts, Sr., landed us an unprecedented live audition with RCA Records.

On March 2, 1983, in the RCA boardroom, Wy and I reached back to our roots, to the very first song we'd learned, "A Mother's Smile." Like the old days on our front porch, our voices came together in perfect harmony. Forty-five minutes later, we were officially RCA recording artists!

Seven years on top of the country music world—that's what Wynonna and I were blessed with. Then in 1990 my body fell apart and I would have too, if I hadn't discovered the third verse of my lifelong song. The symptoms started with headaches and debilitating exhaustion. Some days I couldn't even get out of bed. Wy and I had to cancel one concert after another. Blood tests showed I had hepatitis C, a chronic and sometimes fatal liver disease that I'd most likely contracted from an accidental needle stick in my nursing days.

Treatment with the antiviral drug interferon didn't work, and my weakened system couldn't take the stress of touring. I had no choice. I would have to give up the career I loved. There would be no more making music. No more chasing dreams. *What if you don't live to see your daughters get married?* The fears taunted me. *What if you never know your grandchildren?*

I went right to a children's store and started grabbing christening gowns and baby blankets for Wy and Ashley to save for their kids. Maybe it was touching those things, so concrete and real, that made me remember the song, the faith, that had saved me before. I called our church elders to set up a prayer healing.

That night they anointed me with oil, and I claimed my healing, just like I'd claimed all the other dreams God had put in my heart. *Lord, from now on I will focus not on my illness but on the restoration of my health. On both Wynonna and me coming out of this whole.*

Knowing God had the power to make all of that real, I went on our 1991 Farewell Tour. My liver function continued to be monitored, but no longer with any fear about the results. I took my final bows with Wynonna on December 4, feeling completely at peace.

And so I remain, living in harmony with God's ongoing vision for me. Which is as real as my eleven-year-long remission from hepatitis C. As real as Wy's success as a solo artist and Ashley's as an actress. As real as the books I've written and the TV shows I've done since my "retirement." As real as the Sunday dinners Larry and I have at home at Peaceful Valley, the farm we share with Ashley and her husband, Dario Franchitti, and Wynonna and her two kids, the grandchildren I once thought I would never live to see. As real as the vision that fills my mind, heart and soul—of a loving God with his arms wrapped around my life.

*I sought the Lord, and he heard me,
and delivered me from all my fears.*
—PSALM 34:4

A ROCKY RESCUE

DIANE M. CIARLONI

My mother enthroned Jesus as the Lord and Savior of her life long before I ever heard the term "born-again Christian." The Lord was simply part and parcel of her daily breathing. She invoked his assistance for any task that proved difficult—from the ones that seemed easy but eluded her, right up the ladder to the more complicated ones.

I can remember being no more than seven or eight years old and watching her as she pitted all the strength of her five-foot-tall body into popping the lid from a jar of canned green beans. It wouldn't budge.

Mom stopped and sighed.

Holding the cantankerous jar in her left hand, she raised her eyes heavenward and said, "Lord, I'd like to feed these beans to my family for dinner, but I need your help in getting this lid off. Thank you, Lord."

Her tone was reverential and totally respectful but the little prayer was delivered in an attitude of one friend talking to another. Matter of fact. Affectionate. But, most importantly, confident of receiving an answer.

Mom lowered her eyes and put her right hand on the lid that, just a few seconds earlier, had refused to move so much as one millimeter. She gave a twist and off it came, so easily it appeared oiled.

Even as a youngster, I can remember being impressed by Mom's faith. I believed in her and I believed in God but, for whatever reasons, I just couldn't muster up that closeness she enjoyed. There were times I wondered how in the world she could talk so much to someone she'd never seen. I asked her about it once and she told me she had seen him. Of course, she went on to explain, she saw him in the flowers and trees and stars and a host of his other creations. That was fine, but it wasn't what I had in mind.

Regardless of the closeness I did or did not feel with the Lord, I did grow up knowing there was someone and he was somewhere out there.

Mom didn't read the Bible a lot but she did manage to find various passages relating to horses. You see, I was a horse nut and I had my very own big, black, wonderful Tennessee Walker. His name was Bob's Merry Legs, and he was far more than just a horse. He was a friend. He listened to all the things that welled up inside my secret heart. His broad white blaze caught my tears. His finely etched ears switched back and forth as he strained to catch every syllable I said to him. Mom knew if there was any way to reach me with God, it was through horses.

She read to me passages from Job, with the Lord speaking of the horse's might and majesty. She told me how Jesus would come back one day and he'd be riding on a big, white horse with all his saints riding horseback behind him. I could envision the scene. It made my heart beat faster and my pulse race with excitement. I took it a step farther and mentally seated angels on horses, their robes flowing downward over the strong withers and backward across the muscled rumps. Then, when I went outside with Bob, I pictured him in heaven and thought even Jesus might be proud to ride him.

Every school morning I got out of bed, dressed, ate breakfast and went outside to visit with Bob before catching the yellow school bus that I rode for a total of three hours each day. One morning I went through my routine and then headed for the barn, snatching some sugar cubes as I passed the kitchen counter. I went out the back door whistling and calling for my friend. His routine was as predictable as mine. He would hear my whistle and call, look out the door and then come romping into the paddock to whinny and hang his head over the fence. This particular morning, however, there was something wrong. There was no Bob. It was enough of a deviation that I panicked immediately.

Bob?" I called again. I opened the gate in the paddock and went into the barn. He wasn't there. I went back to the paddock and, from the angle of the barn doorway, I spotted the problem. There was a section of fence down, and Bob had obviously wandered off. I was frightened.

I ran back to the house and told Mom I wouldn't be going to school, a rather presumptuous announcement for a ten-year-old fifth-grader.

"What are you talking about?" she asked.

"Bob's missing."

She didn't repeat what I'd said. Mom was like that. In a crisis she always had an immediate grasp of the situation.

"I'll go get Daddy," she responded. "You wait here."

I could hardly stand still. My best friend was out there somewhere. I knew it would take Mom only a few minutes to drive to the field where Daddy was working in the cotton. That's where I was raised. A one-hundred-acre cotton farm that was crisscrossed with dozens of dirt roads. Bob and I knew all of them.

It seemed like forever, but it couldn't have been more than ten minutes when Daddy pulled into the backyard in his truck with Mom behind in her car.

Mom got out. Daddy didn't. He yelled for me to get in the truck. I ran and he started driving.

We covered those dirt roads, but there was no Bob. He was trying not to show it, but I knew Daddy was getting worried. Suddenly, from nowhere, he said "I'm going across the main dirt road to Mr. Rogers' place." There was something about the way he said it that made my skin prickle. I can still remember it.

We crossed the main road and headed toward a huge gravel pit. Daddy stopped a safe distance from the rim and we got out. We looked down and there, appearing very small, was Bob. I immediately started crying as if my heart had broken.

Today, because there's a lake where the gravel pit was, I know it was more than one hundred feet down and nearly an acre across.

I wiped my eyes, hiccupped three or four times, edged closer to the rim, and looked down. I could see his right rear foot was cocked off the ground, a sure sign that it was injured. There was no use asking or even wondering how or why he'd gotten into the pit. The only concern was getting him out.

We lived in a tiny, rural community. There were no such things as rescue helicopters or anything else bordering on the sophisticated. Daddy began walking around the lip and I followed. He came to a spot that had a more gradual slope than anywhere else. There was a sort of trail leading to the bottom. Bob, who wasn't wearing shoes, had left hoof prints in the dirt that was still semi-soft from a rain three days prior.

Daddy and I looked at one another.

"I have to go down and get him," I said.

"No way," Daddy responded. "You'll get hurt, your mother will kill me and I have no idea what else will happen. But I do know you're not going down there."

I wiped away the last of the tears and looked him in the eye. "Then how will we get him?"

"I'll go," Daddy answered.

"He won't follow you and you know it," I said. "I'll be fine. I can scoot down and, coming up, I'll have Bob to hold on to. He won't let me fall." Suddenly, I knew

I was speaking the truth. Bob was my best friend and that meant I was the one to rescue him; and I was his best friend, which meant he'd do all he could to keep me from harm.

I knew it was a struggle for Daddy, and I know that even more today now that I'm older. I was the youngest of three children, and enjoyed certain privileges that go with being the "baby." Daddy was torn.

"There's no choice, Daddy."

He knew I was right.

"We don't have a lead rope," he said.

"We don't need one. He's wearing a halter. Besides, I know he'll follow me without a rope or a halter."

Daddy knelt down and double-tied my tennis shoes, shortening up on the laces and tightening the knot. He got up and stood back. I knew that was his way of giving permission. I sat down at the top of the trail and started scooting, kicking rocks as I went.

I don't know how long it took to reach the bottom. I was a kid and time wasn't all that important to me. I just remember it seemed to take hours to scoot to the bottom, shredding my jeans in the process.

When I was three-quarters of the way down, Bob hobbled in my direction and started whinnying. I thought of Mama. I knew what she would do.

"Lord," I breathed, "I know I have no business doing this, but my friend needs help. I know you like horses or you wouldn't have them in your Bible. I don't know if I can do this, Lord, so I'd sure appreciate it if you'd give me a hand. Thank you." I didn't know it then, but I must surely have sounded just like Mama.

I reached the bottom and turned around to wave at Daddy. I immediately wished I hadn't done it because it made me think of the climb we'd need to make to get out of the pit. I reached up and patted Bob on the neck.

"You silly, silly horse," I crooned. "Why'd you ever get out and why in the world did you come here?" He looked at me as if to apologize for causing so much trouble.

"Okay," I said, "I know your foot hurts but you don't have a choice—just like I didn't have one. I'll help you but you have to help me too." I took hold of his halter with one hand and put my other hand on the side of his neck to help steady me. We were ready when I suddenly stopped in mid-motion.

"Lord," I said matter-of-factly, "we're going to need all the help you can give us. I'm just a kid and I'm scared. I know Bob's scared, too. Just please don't let us fall, Lord. Just let me and my friend get to the top. Thank you, Lord." I was about to start forward when I stopped again. "Lord," I said, "if you were thinking about sending any angels down here today, it would sure be good if you could send some to go all round us. Maybe they could let us just sort of lean on them. Thanks again."

This time we started up, each step placed slowly and carefully, Bob maneuvering his big bulk along the narrow trail with small rocks scattering from under his feet. I plastered myself as close to him as possible. Every time I extended one foot forward, I can remember saying, "Please, Lord, don't let us fall." I don't know how many times I repeated those words, slipping and going to my knees what seemed like dozens of times. Bob stopped with each slip. I stopped any time he seemed to favor his hurt foot.

We made it to the top. Two best friends holding on to one another. I learned that day what it meant to take risks for a friend and, just as importantly, I learned what kind of relationship I could have with someone I'd never seen. Mama was right . . . as usual. And today, when I can't wrestle the lid from a jar, I simply stop and say, "Lord, I need some help to do this." It never fails, the lid slips off . . . so easily it appears to be oiled.

The
Courage
to
Embrace Life

*Whatever evil befalls us, we ought to ask ourselves . . .
how we can turn it into good. So shall we take occasion from
one bitter root, to raise . . . many flowers.*
—LEIGH HUNT

A BOY WHO LOVED HORSES

WALTER HARTER

When I opened my eyes, a nurse told me I was in the hospital's intensive care unit. Tubes of various sizes sprouted from me, and an oxygen mask covered my mouth and nose. But I didn't care. I felt too ill.

The next time I opened my eyes, a doctor was bending over me. (I later learned he was the surgeon who had operated on me.) He was saying: " . . . think of it as a backup heart. Just like having a second carburetor in your automobile . . . " He probably said more, but I wasn't listening. I was asleep.

Later he explained that when my heart almost stopped beating in the operating room, he had inserted a pacemaker, a small object the size of a pocket watch, that was keeping my heart beating steadily by means of tiny electric shocks.

I tried to remember what had happened.

At the age of seventy I shouldn't have been mowing a large lawn. I had been warned not to exert myself, and I really didn't need to do it, for I could afford to hire someone to get the job done. But I was stubborn.

I remembered black clouds beginning to cover the sky, and I remembered hurrying to get the lawn finished before the rain came. Then nothing. Until I opened my eyes in the intensive care unit.

So that was how I had become a kind of bionic man, kept alive by the ingenuity of modern medical science. I was deeply depressed.

When friends visited me, they showered me with best wishes for a speedy recovery and congratulations on my survival.

Survival for what? My thoughts were that I'd had it. I had reached the pinnacle of three score years and ten. What more should I want or expect? I'd lived longer than most people. I'd had a full life, and I believed I'd helped some people during those years. All I could do now was wait for the inevitable.

As the days passed I could tell that Dr. Hall, who had signed me into the hospital, was getting concerned about my lagging recovery. The pacemaker was operating perfectly. My general health was good. I could walk around my room, and even take short strolls in the corridor. But something was wrong. Something was lacking. I couldn't help thinking that I was in the last act of my life. What was there to look forward to? I became more depressed. I became morbid.

When Dr. Hall visited me again he wasted no words: "You do have a damaged heart. Without modern medicine you'd be dead. But Dr. Haworth [the surgeon] placed a medical wonder in your chest. Therefore you are alive and have a reasonable number of years to live an active life. He's an excellent surgeon and performed his job properly, so why don't you do your part? Stop feeling sorry for yourself. Start living!"

When Dr. Hall left I began my daily stroll down the corridor. What did he know about how I felt? He was twenty years my junior. Let him live another quarter of a century. How would he feel being kept alive by an electric shock every second?

I stepped on something and almost fell. I picked up the object. It was a small plastic horse, no larger than my hand. It had apparently come from room 312, where the door was partly open.

The person in the bed was motioning to me. I pushed open the door and entered. I saw a boy, age nine or ten, propped into a sitting position by pillows.

"He's always running away," the boy said, smiling and reaching for the toy. Over the blanket that covered his legs were dozens of toy horses.

"He's the wild one." The dark eyes in the boy's face made his skin appear even whiter. "I guess he's the leader of the bunch." He smiled at me as though we were sharing a private joke. Not only were toy horses spread over the blanket, but there were books, and all were about horses.

During the next few minutes I learned what was obvious, that horses were his hobby. Listening to the boy talk (and he talked easily and eagerly) and looking at the pictures he showed me in his books, I could imagine horses running, manes flying, and even hear the sound of pounding hooves.

A nurse came in then and I left. Later, I asked one of my nurses about the boy in room 312. I learned that his name was Richard Harris, and he had been in the hospital longer than I had. He too was a cardiac case. A bad one. That was all she knew, or cared to say.

That evening, when I wandered down the hall, the door of room 312 was again ajar, and the boy beckoned to me to enter. He introduced me to his mother, a pleasant woman. We talked a bit and the boy fell asleep. While he dozed, his mother thanked me for visiting her son that morning.

"There are no grandparents on either side," she explained. "I think he has made believe you're one. He has quite an imagination."

The stories he'd told me about horses proved that. And as for imagining me to be a grandfather, well, we'd start even, for I had no grandchildren.

That night, when Dr. Hall made his rounds, I asked about the boy.

"I guess you could call it a paradox," he said. "A pacemaker will keep your old heart ticking, whether you want it or not." He gave me a look that, earlier, would have put my hackles up. "But his young heart, well . . ." He spread his hands. "There's not much there to work with."

"Can't something be done?" I said. "Money . . . ?"

Dr. Hall shook his head. "It's amazing he's still alive. Perhaps when he had rheumatic fever eight years ago—if doctors then had the medicines we have now—perhaps, only perhaps, something could have been done. But he was a frail child, and . . . well, these things do happen."

When he left, my feelings were unsettled, confused. And I felt ashamed. And I did something I'd neglected to do for too many years. I prayed. Not for myself. I hadn't done that even when I was in the intensive care unit, for I hadn't cared if I lived or died. No, I prayed for the boy in Room 312. If he couldn't get well, then, *Please, God, let his passing into your arms be painless and peaceful.*

The next morning I visited the boy again, and though I'd learned that his spells of wakefulness were becoming rarer, and that he slept most of the time, he was now sitting upright in his bed.

Once again we talked about horses. He became animated when he told me about his dream of riding, especially a white horse, the same color as his favorite toy one.

I sensed from some of the things he said that he knew he would never be able to do that. He was aware of why he was in the hospital, and he knew something about hearts. Obviously he had asked the nurses about me, for he was interested in my pacemaker. I explained what I knew about them, and even let him feel the small bulge in my chest that contained the object. It was apparent, though, that his obsession with horses was his way of trying to ignore what, even at his age, he knew to be inevitable.

The next day I checked out of the hospital, to the obvious relief of Dr. Hall. But I still returned to the place at least once each day. There was something that drew me to room 312. Sometimes on those visits the boy was awake; more and more often he was asleep.

But he was awake often enough that we had many talks. I brought him more books about horses and even a large stuffed horse. He thanked me for them, but always his hands returned to the now-battered white horse I had found in the hall.

During those visits I forgot about myself. I felt well, and obviously the pacemaker was continuing to do its work. My concern now was to become the best substitute grandfather in the entire state of Florida. And I worked at it. We developed a friendship that became stronger with each visit.

Then one morning several weeks later, when I appeared at my usual time, I found room 312 empty. Had Richard been taken to some remote part of the hospital for tests? Before I could ask, nurses bustled into the room with a stretcher. The patient was a bearded man, the new occupant of room 312.

A nurse who knew me drew me aside. "Richard died early this morning," she said. "His mother is in the lounge. She thought you might be here about now and she'd like to see you."

Mrs. Harris was pale, but composed. The expected had happened. That was all. She thanked me for my kindnesses to her son, and held out something wrapped in tissue paper. "He wanted you to have this," she said, and walked away.

It was the white plastic horse.

As I hurried from the hospital, a hand grasped my arm. It was Dr. Hall.

"Anything wrong?"

I shook my head and pulled away. I was in a hurry.

"What's the rush?" he called.

I was sure he wouldn't understand, but I told him anyway.

"I'm going to find a horse," I said.

There are lots of horses in St. Augustine. They pull carriages filled with tourists along the palm-shaded streets. They wear funny hats in the annual Easter parade. But the horse I was looking for had to be a special horse. I visited friends who owned horses, and drove into the countryside to farms where horses were raised. I saw black and gray horses, roan and dappled horses, but not one was exactly what I was looking for.

Then, about a month after the boy had died, the search ended. I drove into a farmer's yard and saw a man leading a horse into a stable. The man and horse were both friendly. And when I explained what I wanted to do, the man didn't seem to think it strange at all.

The horse wasn't a fiery steed like those in the pictures the boy had shown me. It was rather elderly. But it was big, and from head to tail it was white!

With the help of the farmer and a stepladder, I managed to mount and sit in the saddle he'd placed on the broad back. I hadn't ridden a horse for almost forty years, and as a seventy-year-old man with a pacemaker, I wasn't about to urge the horse to leap fences and gallop. Elderly man and elderly horse made two rather sedate circuits of the yard.

At the conclusion of the ride I dismounted, again with the aid of helping hand and stepladder.

Driving down the lane to the highway I stopped and looked back. The farmer had led the horse into the stable. The door was pulled shut.

The shutting of the door was like the closing of a book, or the tying up of a loose end. I had done what the boy had wanted to do. The circle was almost closed. But not completely. It wouldn't be, as long as I lived. For some part of that boy would be with me always. I had paid part of the debt I owed to him—and to Someone else. There was living to be done, people to be helped. Riding the white horse was only a down payment.

A wise man turns chance into good fortune.
—THOMAS FULLER

SURVIVING SURVIVAL

JERRY SCHEMMEL

Outside our Denver townhouse the front range of the Rocky Mountains stretched north and south as far as the eye could see. Usually the ragged, snowcapped peaks had a calming effect on me; but now they seemed oppressive, as if their vastness were too much for my mind to handle.

I was sitting in a rocking chair in the bedroom, rocking. I felt as if an insidious paralysis had been smothering my life during the previous nine months, ever since the crash, until my existence was compressed into that one small, steady motion.

I heard my wife, Diane, come in and drop her car keys on the kitchen counter. "Jerry?"

The muted sound of her footsteps on the carpeted stairs almost roused me. *I don't want her coming home to find me like this again.* She walked into the bedroom. "I'm having a really tough time again, honey," I managed to say. Normally Diane would have responded with pity and comfort. That day, though, her embrace was quick, even perfunctory. Diane stood back and waited until our eyes met. "I get my strength from God," she said, then left the room.

She didn't say it smugly or accusingly but almost as if giving me the final, matter-of-fact clue to my way out of the terrible maze I had stumbled through since that day aboard a DC-10 when I had plunged, along with the 295 other passengers, including my best friend, thirty-six thousand feet into an Iowa cornfield.

I was the last passenger to board United Flight 232 from Denver to Chicago on July 19, 1989. My partner, Jay Ramsdell, and I were determined to make the flight after having been bumped off several others that morning. Jay, age twenty-five and four years my junior, was the dynamic young commissioner of the Continental Basketball Association, a kind of minor league for the big-time National Basketball Association. I was his deputy commissioner, general counsel, and friend. We needed to get to Columbus, Ohio, for the annual CBA player draft, and Flight 232 was our last hope.

Jay was assigned to 30J and I sat in 23G. Looking around at all the young families traveling in the heart of summer-vacation season, I realized I wouldn't get much sleep on the trip. I decided to catch up on some paperwork. Less than an hour into the flight an explosion ripped through the tail of the aircraft.

Instinctively, I grabbed the armrest, spilling my coffee on the tray table. I felt the plane drop slightly—not a sudden movement but more a loss of stability. Then we banked heavily right. My overturned coffee cup flew off the tray. People screamed. Then fear caught in my throat and I realized I was actually trying to say, "Good-bye, Diane. I love you."

Minutes passed before my grip on the armrest relaxed. Whatever was going to happen to us was not going to happen right away. I said a prayer, probably not a very good one. But I was profoundly grateful my wife of four years was safe on the ground. I thanked God she did not have to share this terror.

Clearly the crew was having trouble flying the big DC-10. After one announcement asking for calm, Captain Al Haynes explained that the cockpit had lost most of the ability to control the plane and we would be forced to attempt an emergency landing at the Sioux City, Iowa, airport. There was a ripple of gasps and a few sobs. Later he came back on and said he would make an announcement thirty seconds before impact warning us to brace. "And folks," he added, "I'm not going to kid anyone. This is going to be rough."

The flight attendants briefed us on crash procedures. I double-checked the location of the emergency exit. In front of me sat Sylvia Tsao and her son, Evan, age 21 months. I made them a priority. I would find them immediately after landing and make sure they got to safety. Once more I prayed, trying to make my peace. Aching regret crept in, regret for the children Diane and I might never have, regret that my dream of becoming an NBA play-by-play announcer might never be. But mostly I felt ready to face death.

I had tried to catch Jay's eye several times since the explosion some forty minutes earlier, but he had been talking earnestly to the person next to him. Intuitively I turned my head again. Jay was staring straight at me. He smiled and gave me a thumbs-up.

Captain Haynes's voice boomed over the PA speaker: "Brace, brace, brace!" Thirty seconds. I glanced out the window at the bright-blue summertime sky, like the midwestern skies of my boyhood. So peaceful. I felt an incredible, pulverizing jolt, and a terrible sound came from all around me. I remember the irresistible momentum of tremendous force, and cries in the now dark cabin. I tried to grip the seat in front of me, Sylvia's. Gone. A man's body flew past. A woman still strapped in her seat shot by, followed by a storm of debris and a ball of fire. Pain exploded through my back. Then, all at once, the entire aircraft went into an end-over-end cartwheel.

I was dangling upside down when the plane finally came to a rest. I don't remember how I got my seat belt undone but somehow I found myself standing on the cabin ceiling, which was then the floor. Flames faintly illuminated a scene of ghastly carnage. Moans thickened the smoky air. Amazingly, there were others stumbling around. Alive, dying, and dead, people dangled from the seats above me. Where were Sylvia and Evan? Jay? *Help the others*, I kept thinking. Then a bolt of sunlight split the gloom. People were escaping through a gap in the fuselage and all at once I knew I would survive.

I began helping people move toward the light. I grabbed a woman heading dazedly the wrong way. Sylvia Tsao. "I'm not leaving without my son!" she screamed.

"You've got to go. Now! I'll find him."

She turned back and I scanned the rubble. The flames were building and the cabin was filling with acrid smoke. "We've got to get out," a man shouted to me urgently. He and I were the last two people to leave the burning portion of the fuselage.

I stepped into a cornfield, a good quarter mile from the runway. People were moving quickly through the tall stalks. I was poised to take off running, but a muffled sound from the wreckage—an infant's cry—froze me in my tracks. I turned.

"Don't go back in there," someone said.

I'm no hero. I didn't decide to go back into that burning airliner. I just went.

I can't recall much of it. I was in the plane, following the sound. *Don't stop crying*, I thought. I lifted shattered overhead-storage bins lying at my feet. Burning smoke was everywhere. I stopped above the spot where the crying was loudest, pulled away some debris, and picked up an infant.

Then I was wandering in the cornfield again, carrying a tiny baby girl in a light-blue dress, the color of the sky. She gave me a beautiful smile and I knew she was all right. I handed her to someone. I whirled around and ran back toward the wreckage. But flames engulfed everything and I couldn't even get close.

Nearly ten months later I found myself in the rocking chair, alone in the bedroom, Diane's words hanging in the air. *I get my strength from God.* I had survived the crash of Flight 232, but would I survive survival?

In the hours following the disaster I was interviewed by news organizations and television reporters. I thought Jay, who had been listed as missing, might have somehow wandered away from the crash scene. There had been such chaos. Pieces of the plane had been scattered over a huge area. Maybe someone had seen Jay. My desperation turned to grief as I accepted the fact he had not made it out, had probably not even survived impact. Nor had Evan Tsao. Nor had 110 others.

Why had I?

That was the question that followed me like a shadow. My best friend, a brilliant guy, was dead. We had walked side by side for most of that day and had been seated seven rows apart, a distance of about only thirty feet. Yet his life was over and mine went on. I couldn't understand it. The media called me a hero. People stopped me on the street. The little girl I had carried out had been reunited with her parents. Yet I had made Evan Tsao my responsibility and he was dead. It seemed so arbitrary.

I left my job at the CBA a few months after the crash; the strong sense of motivation that had always driven my professional life was replaced by apathy. I sought relief in running, and spent a lot of time by myself. The more Diane tried to help me, the more I pushed her away. Finally I agreed to see a trauma counselor.

"Jerry, you're suffering from depression," she said at the end of the session.

Depression? I had walked away from a horrifying plane crash with not much more than a few bruises and whiplash. I had cheated death. What did I have to be depressed about? Still, it felt as if a part of me had died on that plane. Night after night my sleep was tortured with dreams of people trying to escape the burning cabin and wandering through a cornfield. I had always been proud of the way I handled conflict. I would identify my problem, assess my options, decide on a course of action, and follow through. Now it wasn't working. Nothing was working.

Slumped in the rocker in the pale dusk, I stared at the bedroom doorway through which Diane had just left. The more depressed I became, the more she had studied her Bible. We had gone to church and prayed together and cried together. But as things deteriorated, so had my relationship with God, a God in whom I had always believed yet had never fully trusted with my life even as that plane plummeted to Earth.

Suddenly I felt that if I didn't turn to him right at that moment, in complete faith, as Diane had, I might never get up from the rocker. I felt as close to death as I had been in seat 23G.

I closed my eyes, bowed my head and asked God to come into my life once and for all. *Give me some relief from this battle and this pain, Lord. Please. I surrender.*

Not an instant elapsed before an overwhelming sensation of pure energy filled my body. At the same time I was utterly calm, utterly at peace. I had never known such peace. I sensed that never again would I be the person I had been a moment or a year before.

I got up from the chair and went to Diane. I held her closer than I had ever held her and let my tears streak her hair. I had fallen thirty-six thousand feet in a DC-10—and a lot further into depression and despair—to finally find God. I didn't realize God was all I needed until God was all I had left.

Post-traumatic depression doesn't disappear overnight. Slowly I rebuilt my life. I fulfilled my dream when I became the play-by-play announcer for the Denver Nuggets. Jay would have been proud. Diane and I have a beautiful daughter, Maggie.

Every survivor of Flight 232 was a miracle and every victim a tragedy. I cannot explain why I survived and Jay didn't. My task, I have found, isn't to understand but to accept. The crash changed my life forever, and in mostly good ways—not because tragedy is good, but because God uses the worst moments of our lives as ways to grow us closer to him.

Acceptance of what has happened is the first step to overcoming the consequences of any misfortune.
—WILLIAM JAMES

LESSONS

CRYSTAL WARD KENT

Sooner or later everyone has their "dark night of the soul," that time when they question their beliefs and their will to go on. Mine came on March 13, 1987, as my sister, Laurel, lay dying of a vicious virus.

No one expects a twenty-nine-year-old girl to die, and if death does come to one so young, you expect it to be from a car accident, not a sudden illness. You never believe that what seemed like the flu will turn out to be viral meningitis, a silent killer that can destroy all vital organs in twenty-four hours. But this was the reality. This was my sister lying in the ICU.

My sister and I grew up close. We shared a room, shared clothes, shared secrets. From our earliest days together we were friends, playmates, and each other's supporter. There weren't many kids in our neighborhood during our early childhood, so Laurel and I were lucky to have each other. We played Barbies and baby dolls, galloped our toy horses throughout the house, rode bikes, and whirled hula hoops. Our grandmother and great-aunt lived next door, and we were frequent visitors, often playing dress-up in their old clothes or having tea parties under the trees. We did everything together—Scouts, dance lessons, baton lessons. We frequently giggled under the covers long past bedtime, swapping jokes and silly stories.

As we grew older, we moved into separate but adjacent rooms with a shared bath. True to form, as the older sister I was the leader, the protector. I paved the way through all the firsts: first day of school, first date, first to drive. "Your sister really looks up to you," was a common refrain from my parents, and I took the role of big sister seriously. When Laurel was afraid to go underwater after a bad incident at summer camp, I worked with her all one summer to teach her to swim and eventually to go under again. I taught her to draw, coached her on her writing and her fashion sense. I introduced her to my friends and gave her the low-down on teachers, courses, and boys. We frequently socialized; my friends were hers and vice versa. We even double-dated on occasion. We chose to attend the same college, and even wound up in the same dorm, although we didn't share a room. I introduced her to the challenges of life at school: the best dining halls, the worst courses, the dryer that burned your underwear, the must-have furnishings for your room. Not that we didn't fight—Laurel had a fiery temper (her nickname was "Spitfire")—and we were equally stubborn. Screaming and door slams were not unknown, but in the end, we always made up.

It was easy to be protective of Laurel. She was also very short and extremely near-sighted. Standing barely five feet tall (and always standing very straight so every one of those sixty inches counted), Laurel had begun wearing glasses in third grade. By high school, she was legally blind without her glasses. When we went to the beach, she took them off to go swimming, and I would have to guide her back to our blanket. Later, she got contacts, but it was still scary how poor her vision was without them.

Through the years there were countless times when I came to the rescue—to apply cold compresses when a bad sunburn kept her from sleeping, to get a basin when she was sick in the night, to help with a last-minute term paper, or listen as she sobbed over a broken romance. After awhile, you think you will always be there to "fix" things. As the "big sister," there isn't any problem you can't solve, any battle you can't win. But this time, the battle was too big.

As I stood in the ICU gazing down at Laurel, I felt detached. The whole scenario was unreal. Only yesterday, we had been making plans for our first-ever vacation together. We were going to Disney World. I could still hear her voice on the phone, "I can't believe what a trip we have!" she exclaimed. We were setting dates to go clothes shopping, and to a basketball game. She had called me at work, but I had to cut the conversation short because an appointment had arrived. I didn't realize it would be the last time I would hear her voice.

Now, here I was, gowned from head to toe in sterile garments to protect me from her virus. I could only touch her with gloves on. Laurel lay on a gurney, tubes everywhere, including a tube mainlining antibiotics into her carotid artery. Ugly purple splotches colored her arms, symptomatic of the meningitis. I looked at her hand, still small as a child's, yet with brightly painted nails. I noticed her temperature was dropping and at first thought this was a good sign, that her fever was abating, but when I voiced this, and saw the nurses' eyes, I knew the truth. Her body was cooling because she was dying. We were losing the battle. I spoke to Laurel softly, but I did not sense her there. She had not yet been declared dead, but deep in my soul, I felt she was gone.

I returned to the waiting room where my parents, some close family members, and the minister were all locked in prayer. I couldn't stay there amid the desperation. I needed to be alone and wage my private fight. At home, I sat in our darkened living room. Our animals, three cats, silently filed in and sat facing me. They knew. We all sat there, waiting, for what I don't know. For the end to be declared? For the miracle to occur? My mind still couldn't fathom the situation and my thoughts drifted back to how the nightmare began.

The afternoon before, my sister had lunch with my mom, but ate lightly because she felt "odd." A few hours later, she went home from work feeling ill. She had a date that night which she canceled. Early the next day, she called my mom, saying she had been up all night vomiting and guessed she needed to go to the emergency room. Mom took her, and once there they were able to calm her stomach. She was talking and joking and about to be dismissed, when the doctor came back and voiced some concern. As part of the procedure, they had done blood work and checked her blood pressure. She had a very high white cell count and her blood pressure was very low. Unknown to all of us, and to her, a deadly virus had invaded her body sometime within the past few days. How she got it we'll never know for sure, but constant ear infections and strep throat are frequent pathways for meningitis, and my sister had been plagued with both. March is also the month when meningitis is at its peak, and her health conditions left her vulnerable. As the doctor scheduled a spinal tap, my sister broke out in the telltale purple rash and began complaining of headache. Within another hour, she had slipped into a coma. She never woke up.

Meanwhile, I was at home. The last I had heard, Laurel was on her way to recuperate with us. When I got the call that she was deathly ill, I was in shock. I quickly called family and friends and asked for prayers. Two churches activated prayer chains. I was sure God would prevail, but ten hours later, I knew he would not—or not in the way I had hoped. Despite some last-ditch heroics, Laurel was declared dead on March 14.

The days after her death were a blur of funeral preparations, phone calls, cleaning out her apartment, and seeing to her personal affairs. Everyone was in shock. Here was a young woman who only days before had been a busy paralegal, had a calendar packed with activity, had a life. Yet a disease had attacked her out of the blue and struck her down. Helping her friends adjust allowed me to get through those early days, but within a few weeks things had slowed down. Now there was time to think, to be angry, to wonder why God hadn't heard the many prayers launched at him. What possible good could come from taking this vibrant young woman with so much to give? I felt desolation creep into my soul. I had trusted God to see Laurel through. I had counted on the prayer chains to save her. What had gone wrong? Finding no answer, I threw myself into my work. My relationship with God was on hold.

A few months later I had dinner with Anne, one of Laurel's best friends and former college roommate. I knew Anne missed Laurel terribly. She was about to have her first child and she and Laurel had been very excited about shopping for the nursery and sharing baby plans. Now that would never take place. I expected Anne to share my outrage, but while she grieved, she showed no anger. "I think Laurel got a better offer," she said calmly. "I think she was deeply troubled and God knew this. I don't think he sent the illness, but when it occurred, I think he offered her a chance to come to him and she did. Think about it," she continued. "Meningitis almost always leaves a mark—brain impairment, blindness, a weakened heart. And Laurel was stricken by a very severe case. Yes, she might have lived, but she probably would not have been as she was. You also know she had a lot of concerns in her life at the time of her death. I think when she was given a chance to be at peace, to be healthy and whole in another life, she took it. I think of her like that—happy, at ease—and I can accept."

I sat in silence. I had not thought of Laurel wanting to leave. I guess we always think in terms of what we want, what is easiest for us, the living. I knew Laurel was going through a tough time. A young man she truly loved had turned out to be a drug addict and an alcoholic. He kept promising to mend his ways, but the promises were empty. She had done everything in her power to get him help, but the lure of his friends was too powerful. Now, in a last-ditch attempt to keep her, he had offered marriage. Because she loved him, Laurel wanted to say "yes," but in her heart, she knew that would only lead to a life of misery. She had written him a letter turning him down, yet saying she believed one day he would have the strength to come clean. She promised to love him always. She had planned to mail the letter the day she died.

I knew it had cost Laurel to write that letter. I knew how she had agonized over doing it and what to say. I knew it would have been very hard for her to stick to her promise not to see him until he was free of his addictions. I also knew that what Anne had said about the meningitis was true, and the thought of Laurel blind or mentally impaired was horrifying. Perhaps while we had waged our battle for her life she had accepted the chance to move on, to be free of earthly troubles and assured of a new start in a better place.

I did not accept Anne's belief all at once. Her faith was deeper than mine. I still had too much anger and too much pain. But she had planted a seed. In time, I started talking to God again. I started out slowly, a prayer in the morning, a prayer at night. I read spiritual articles for inspiration and gradually saw how others had found their way back. Later, I began keeping a prayer journal. As time passed, I began to see how God did answer prayers, large and small—and how sometimes his not answering them was for the best. I didn't understand everything, but I could feel my mind and my heart opening up again.

I also discovered that while I still missed my sister desperately, the pain was not as intense. I could laugh again, have fun, could even talk about her and our good times without tears. Life was going on; maybe not the life I thought I would have, but it was a good life in its own way.

Three years after Laurel's death I made a huge decision. I quit my corporate job to start my own business. Knowing how suddenly life can change, I was determined to make every day count. I wanted more time with my family, my pets, and my friends. I wanted the freedom to do what I wanted to do, to work on things that I felt were important and not be so caught up in corporate politics and bureaucracy. In most ways, I do not regret the decision. It has not been easy financially and sometimes I have had misgivings over that, but emotionally and creatively it has been very rewarding.

Because I can make my own hours, I have been able to enjoy time caring for my niece, Sarah Laurel, and my nephew, Tommy. I would not have traded that time for all the money in the world. I have had the chance to say "I love you" each and every day to the people I love most, and, believe me, I know how vital that is. I have been able to seize a glorious morning and tramp the woods with my dog, or play hooky on a hot summer afternoon and revel in the glory of July. I have been able to take time to have tea parties with a dear little girl under the trees, or sit in a berry patch and introduce a small boy to the delight of fresh strawberries. Time wasted? I haven't thought so. In the grand scheme of things, these have been the most important times in my life. Laurel's passing taught me to rejoice in each day, and for that knowledge I am grateful.

I will never stop wishing that meningitis had not touched our family, and that Laurel was still here sharing this life. But I have come to believe that good can come out of pain. We can never see what the future holds, and we cannot ensure its path is what we would wish, but with faith, we can go on, and that makes all the difference.

Nothing is miserable unless you think it so.
—BOETHIUS

THE DAY THE TWISTER HIT

SHERRY L. CRAW

Early that morning—while it was still pitch-black outside—a tornado swept through our town and changed our lives forever.

I'd lived in central Illinois, known as "tornado alley," all my life, so tornado watches and warnings were routine. Most locals never really took them seriously. Perhaps that's why, despite a tornado watch posted until midnight, as a thunderstorm noisily boomed outside my home, I felt safe and secure inside.

It was March 27, 1998, the Friday night of spring break, and my husband, Dan, and I had given our two daughters, Meridan, nine, and Emery, five, permission to sleep on the family-room floor overnight. The girls fell asleep around 11:00 P.M., and Dan went to bed around midnight. I stayed on the couch in the family room, quietly watching TV, and nodded off, awakened by howling winds at 12:45 A.M.

Should I stay down here on the couch with the girls? I wondered. I decided against it, knowing my back would ache the following day if I didn't go up to bed. By 1:00 A.M. I was upstairs, sound asleep.

Four hours later, a loud explosion jarred us both awake. Dan and I bolted up in our bed and peeked out the window. There was an eerie green glow in the darkness. Dan, suspecting a tornado, yelled for me to get up. (Later, I discovered that the explosion we heard was our next-door neighbor's minivan being picked up, moved across the street, and slammed down on its side.)

I have to get to the girls! I thought, panicking as our house shook and glass shattered everywhere. As I headed down the stairs, I prayed, *God, please give me the peace that passes all understanding RIGHT NOW!* Instantly I felt a peace I'd never felt before; it was as though God were present in that stairway. I ran down the stairs as fast as I could, in complete darkness, barefoot over broken glass, and never sustained even a scratch.

Before I reached the bottom of the stairs, I heard the sound of a roaring freight train—often associated with a tornado. That's when the reality of our situation hit home.

At the bottom of the stairs, I turned toward the family room where Meridan and Emery were—just as the tornado tore off the north wall of our family room. I looked directly through the tornado to the apartment building next door. Thank goodness, the girls appeared unharmed—but the couch I'd been sleeping on just five hours earlier was covered in glass and debris. If I'd stayed there, I could have been injured or possibly sucked into the tornado.

As debris swirled in a funneling motion, the darkness became as bright as midmorning. Just as quickly, it passed; darkness returned. Time seemed suspended as Dan and I herded the girls into the dining room, the safest place in our basementless house. As the rumbling passed our house, we huddled there.

"Mom, Dad—are we going to die?" Meridan and Emery, frightened, asked. I heard myself telling them we were alive, that nothing else mattered. It was as though someone else—God—were speaking through me. When Emery asked if our things were okay, I said, "I don't know, baby, but it doesn't matter. Things can be replaced—but lives can't. We're alive, and God's right here with us."

I realized then I truly didn't care about our material possessions. We could do without anything—we were together, and that's what mattered.

Emery, who had been lying on the floor next to Meridan, escaped injury. But Meridan had a cut on her back and a possible broken shoulder. Before we could seek help, two neighbors, one of whom we didn't even know, were there inside our house, helping us get Meridan to the hospital. As we got into our neighbor's car, Dan flagged down an ambulance, which was able to wind through the downed power lines and debris to reach the hospital emergency room.

As I walked to the ambulance, I paused a moment to look at our home. Our shed, our garage, and half our house were gone; our vehicles were buried under a pile of rubble. Although I was in shock over what had just happened, the peace I'd prayed for in the stairway still lingered.

Once in the emergency room, the doctor discovered that Meridan's cut was minor, her shoulder was dislocated but not broken, and she had a punctured lung. Meridan was in the hospital for three and a half days, then was released. She's since made a full recovery. We found out the following day that Meridan was the most severely injured victim of the tornado—a miracle in itself. Our whole block was hit, and several houses were destroyed. Like us, almost everyone had been asleep, with no time to take cover.

When the insurance adjuster came to look at our house, he discovered the entire back had been torn apart, the walls had been separated and bowed out, the structure had shifted on the foundation, and the top leaned to one side. He told us that if the tornado had stayed at our house just one or two seconds longer, the entire structure would have collapsed on top of us. God's timing protected us to within a second!

We were only dislocated for two months after the tornado. We lost our home on March 28, and bought our new home on May 29. Now we're settled and getting on with our lives. God also provided me with a new job with flexible hours so I can spend more time with our girls. Because of the tornado, I had so much paperwork to do at our bank—dealing with the insurance settlement, paying off our old mortgage, getting a new one approved—that the bank manager offered me a job. God's provided for our financial needs, and I've even had a few opportunities to share my relationship with Jesus Christ with my coworkers.

After the tornado we were nervous whenever it got stormy outside. But as time goes on, God's healing that part of our lives, too. We've chosen not to live in fear but to be thankful every day for what we have and where God's brought us. We know now that if God decides to take away all or part of what he's given to us, that's okay. All we have is God's, anyway.

Someone asked me why, since we're Christians, God allowed the tornado to hit our house. My response was, "Why not us?" While I'd certainly never wish for a tornado or other disaster, I would not trade the blessings God's given. My relationship with Dan and the girls has never been closer. And while God's restored our material possessions, the one thing that's most important—my relationship with him—is deeper than ever before. For that, I am forever thankful.

Do not weep; do not wax indignant. Understand.
—BARUCH SPINOZA

MISSING BEN

ANDREA WARREN

Jay was always aware of the telltale signs before I was. Shortly after Thanksgiving, I would become distracted, my normally easygoing outlook tinged with gloom, tears ever closer to the surface.

"You get like this every year," my husband said in exasperation last November, sitting on the bed where I lay teary-eyed. "I do everything I can think of to make you feel better, but nothing works. It's no fun for either of us anymore. Is it always going to be this way?" When I didn't reply, he left the room.

In my misery, I thought, *He simply doesn't understand*—though if anyone understood, it was Jay. But he couldn't make Christmas okay for me. No one could.

In 1986, Brendon (Ben), my ten-year-old son and the stepson Jay had loved deeply for seven years, was hit by a car and killed. I had hated the holidays ever since. While I missed Ben every day, his loss was keenest at this time of year, with its emphasis on celebration, joy, and family togetherness. For years after Ben's death, I went through the motions of a happy Christmas for the sake of our other three children: my daughter and Jay's daughter, as well as his son, who didn't live with us. I kept my spirits up for them while grieving in private for their younger brother. But now that our daughters were in their twenties and lived away from home, my holiday depression had resurfaced with a vengeance. I wanted to turn back time. I wanted my little boy back so we could experience the wonder and joy of Christmas again, the way it was before our family was plunged into anguish by a tragic moment on a busy street.

As I wrestled with my feelings, I realized that I didn't want to ruin another holiday season for Jay. I owed him more than that. But did I even have it within me to feel the spirit of Christmas once again?

One evening several days later, I was talking to one of my daughters over the phone when I mentioned how much Ben had been on my mind. For a moment, there was silence. Then she spoke, her voice breaking with emotion: "I've been thinking about him too. Ever since he died, I've just wanted to get Christmas over with."

Her words jolted me. All those years, I thought the girls had still had a good time celebrating the holidays. Had they just been putting on an act for my sake? Had they, too, become incapable of enjoying what I knew deep in my heart could be the happiest, best time of year?

I had thought that somehow, as the years passed, I would naturally begin to anticipate the holiday season again. As I hung up the phone, I realized that time couldn't make this happen; Ben would always be missing from our lives, and we would always feel his loss most acutely at this time of year. But if I could acknowledge my grief instead of stifling it, and honor my son's memory at the same time, perhaps I could find joy in the holidays again—which meant Jay could, too. Then we might be able to help our daughters rekindle their own Christmas spirit.

After much thought, I told Jay I wanted this year to be different, that I didn't want to spend December under a cloud of gloom. I could see the relief in his eyes as he offered to do whatever he could to help me. We came up with a plan that we hoped would work for both of us.

First, we would work at finding pleasure in all that was magical and wonderful about the holidays. Second, we would speak of Ben whenever he came to mind—no holding back for fear of depressing ourselves or others. Finally, we would do one special thing to commemorate how much we missed our son. All three, it turned out, were important.

Starting with the first goal, I concentrated on engaging my senses to the fullest. For the past ten years, I realized, I had shut them down, numbing myself to the twinkle of lights, the sound of carols, the smell of evergreen, the tastes of mint, almond, arid ginger. Now I embraced them. I also gave more thought to each holiday task—from wrapping presents to mailing cards—appreciating them as time-honored rituals instead of dreary chores to be gotten out of the way.

I unpacked several paper-and-paste ornaments Ben had made in grade school, including a primitive little yarn frame with his school picture in it. Closing my eyes, I ran my fingers over the aging wool and the small image of Ben with his happy, gap-toothed grin, a child who loved the Chicago Cubs, books, cats and dogs, silly sayings. After the accident, I had stored these precious creations away, unable to bear looking at them. But our son had made them for us, to be displayed and admired. We hung them on the tree. From now on, we would bring them out, touch them, and allow them to touch us.

Several weeks before Christmas, I had lunch with a friend I had not seen for many months. She dwelled at length on how much she hated the holidays—too much rich food, too many expectations. Then she lamented feeling "deserted" because her newly married son would be spending the holidays with his wife's family.

The old me would have nodded while inwardly screaming, *At least you have your son. Look at me; your pain is nothing compared to mine!* But I had vowed not to keep quiet when Ben was on my mind. I took a deep breath and forced myself to sympathize with her. Then, measuring my words carefully, I told her that I was trying hard to enjoy the holidays in spite of how much I still missed Ben.

My friend looked startled, and for a moment I regretted saying anything. Then she put her hand on my arm. Her eyes were moist. "I think this is the first time since Ben's death that you've mentioned him to me," she said. "Whenever I started to say something about him, I could tell you didn't want to talk about it, so I assumed you must be over your grief. But now I know. . . ." Her words caught in her throat. "You've just given me a special gift. I'm going to be grateful for what I have and stop complaining."

I nevertheless would have given anything to be able to commiserate with her about our adult sons, but at least I had finally spoken. And in breaking my silence at long last, I let my friend draw me close.

A few days later while out shopping, Jay and I stopped in a busy café for espresso. There, I was suddenly reminded of one Christmas we had spent nursing Ben through the flu. As I recalled this to Jay, tears welled in his eyes, then in mine. "I miss him so much," he whispered. There, amid the bustle of holiday shoppers, we held hands under the table, let our tears fall, and managed to smile at each other, enriched by our shared remembrance and our love.

We were discussing how best to accomplish our third goal of honoring Ben's memory—a special holiday concert, perhaps?—when we saw a notice in the local newspaper about "A Service of Remembrance: In Memory of Those We Miss the Most at Christmas." Jay and I didn't belong to that church's denomination, but no matter. We gathered with a hundred other bereaved souls, and in a lovely, quiet, candlelight service, we listened to comforting words and beautiful music, including the haunting song "I Miss You Most at Christmastime." Then we put the names of the people we had loved and lost into a special basket on the altar.

My tears felt especially healing that night, and I entered the busy final week before Christmas with a sense of peace that had eluded me in years past. Over the phone, we shared our feelings with our daughters and offered heartfelt support as they expressed their own sadness about Ben. When we wished them Merry Christmas, I felt we all could truly have one at last.

On December 25, Jay and I toasted our families and the memory of Ben at a family gathering in my brother's home in Nashville. When January 2 arrived, I realized that for the first time in ten years, I had actually enjoyed Christmas. It would never be what it was, but it could still be good. I felt that Ben would be pleased.

This year, with the holidays approaching, I am aware once again of my sadness for what cannot be, but I am focusing on what I still have and what is worth celebrating. For the bereaved, whether our losses be new or old, our challenge is to be happy in the moment, to see the star, to celebrate the magic of the season, and to cherish the memory of our departed loved ones.

Persevering in Times of Trouble

Whoever falls from God's right hand is caught into his left.
—EDWIN MARKHAM

KEEPING FAITH

JOHN MCCAIN WITH MARK SALTER

Our senior officers always stressed to us the three essential keys to resistance, which we were to keep uppermost in our mind, especially in moments when we were isolated or otherwise deprived of their guidance and the counsel of other prisoners. They were faith in God, faith in country, and faith in your fellow prisoners.

Were your faith in any of these three devotions seriously shaken, you became much more vulnerable to various pressures employed by the Vietnamese to break you. The purpose of our captors' inhumanity to us was nothing less than to force our descent into a world of total faithlessness; a world with no God, no country, no loyalty. Our faith would be replaced with simple reliance on the sufferance of our antagonists. Without faith, we would lose our dignity, and live among our enemies as animals lived among their human masters.

There were times in many a prisoner's existence when the Vietnamese came close to robbing his faith; when a prisoner felt abandoned, left to cling to faith in himself as his last strength, his last form of resistance. Certainly this had been my experience when I was broken in the fall of 1968.

Ironically for someone who had so long asserted his own individuality as his first and best defense against insults of any kind, I discovered that faith in myself proved to be the least formidable strength I possessed when confronting, alone, organized inhumanity on a greater scale than I had conceived possible. Faith in myself was important, and remains important to my self-esteem. But I discovered in prison that faith in myself alone, separate from other, more important allegiances, was ultimately no match for the cruelty that human beings could devise when they were entirely unencumbered by respect for the God-given dignity of man. This is the lesson I learned in prison. It is, perhaps, the most important lesson I have ever learned.

During the worst moments of captivity, keeping our faith in God, country, and one another was as difficult as it was imperative. When your faith weakened, you had to take any opportunity, seize on any sight of it, and use any temporary relief from your distress to recover it.

POWs often regard their prison experience as comparable to the trials of Job. Indeed, for my fellow prisoners who suffered more than I, the comparison is appropriate. Hungry, beaten, hurt, scared, and alone, human beings can begin to feel that they are removed from God's love, a vast distance separating them from their Creator. The anguish can lead to resentment, to the awful despair that God has forsaken you.

To guard against such despair, in our most dire moments, POWs would make supreme efforts to grasp our faith tightly, to profess it alone, in the dark, and hasten its revival. Once I was thrown into another cell after a long and difficult interrogation. I discovered scratched into one of the cell's walls the creed "I believe in God, the Father Almighty." There, standing witness to God's presence in a remote, concealed place, recalled to my faith by a stronger, better man, I felt God's love and care more vividly than I would have felt it had I been safe among a pious congregation in the most magnificent cathedral.

The Vietnamese also went to great lengths to sow doubts in our minds about our country and one another. They threatened us constantly that we would never again be free. They taunted us with insults, disparaged our loyalty to a country they claimed never asked about us or made our return the subject of negotiations. We were abandoned, they insisted, by a country busy with a war that wasn't going well and too torn apart by widespread domestic turmoil to worry about a few forgotten pilots in Hanoi.

During the long pause between bombing campaigns in the North, while the months and years dragged on, it was hard to take our interrogators' ridicule of our conviction that our loyalty to America was returned, measure for measure, by our distant compatriots. But we clung to our belief, each one encouraging the other, not with overexuberant hopes that our day of liberation was close at hand, but with a steady resolve that our honor was the extension of a great nation's honor, and that both prisoner and country would do what honor asked of us.

In prison, I fell in love with my country. I had loved her before then, but like most young people, my affection was little more than a simple appreciation for the comforts and privileges most Americans enjoyed and took for granted. It wasn't until I had lost America for a time that I realized how much I loved her.

I loved what I missed most from my life at home: my family and friends, the sights and sounds of my country, the hustle and purposefulness of Americans, their fervid independence, sports, music, information—all the attractive qualities of American life. But though I longed for the things at home I cherished the most, I still shared the ideals of America. And since those ideals were all that I possessed of my country, they became all the more important to me.

It was what freedom conferred on America that I loved the most—the distinction of being the last, best hope of humanity; the advocate for all who believed in the rights of man. Freedom is America's honor, and all honor comes with obligations. We have the obligation to use our freedom wisely, to select well from all the choices freedom offers. We can accept or reject the obligation, but if we are to preserve our freedom, our honor, we must choose well.

I was no longer the boy to whom liberty meant simply that I could do as I pleased, and who, in my vanity, used my freedom to polish my image as a nonconformist. That's not to say that I had shed myself entirely of that attribute. I had not, and have not yet. But I no longer located my self-respect in that distinction. In prison, where my cherished independence was mocked and assaulted, I found my self-respect in a shared fidelity to my country. All honor comes with obligations. I and the men with whom I served had accepted ours, and we were grateful for the privilege.

When my interrogators played tapes to me of other POWs confessing to war crimes, expressing their gratitude for lenient treatment, or denouncing our government, I did not silently censure my comrades. I knew that they had made those statements under the most extreme duress, and I told the Vietnamese so.

"No, they are their true feelings," the interrogator would rebut, "and you should not be ashamed to state your true feelings. We will not tell anyone if you do. No one would know."

"I would know. I would know," I responded.

In these instances when the enemy entreated me to betray my country by promising to keep my disloyalty confidential, my self-regard, which had for so long been invested with an adolescent understanding of my father's and grandfather's notions of character, obliged me to resist. But there was another force now at work to brace my resolve, and to give me insight into the essence of courage in war.

Tom Kirk, a fellow prisoner whom I hold in high regard, once explained, simply and exactly, the foundation of our resistance. "You live with another guy, and you go over there and you're tortured and you're brought back in that room and he says: 'What happened?'

" 'They did this.'

" 'What'd you tell them?'

". . . You've got to face this guy; you're going to have to tell him the truth. I wanted to keep faith so that I knew that when I stood up at the bar with somebody after the war, that I could look him in the eye and say, 'We hacked it.' "

We were told to have faith in God, country, and one another. Most of us did. But the last of these, faith in one another, was our final defense, the ramparts our enemy could not cross. In prison, as in any of war's endeavors, your most important allegiance is to the men you serve with. We were obligated to one another, and for the duration of our war, that obligation was our first duty. The Vietnamese knew this. They went to great lengths to keep us apart, knowing we had great strength in unity.

A few men lost their religion in prison or had never been very devout. A few men were not moved by appeals to patriotism or to written codes of conduct. Almost all of us were committed to one another. I knew what the others were suffering. Sitting in my cell, I could hear their screams as their faith was put to the test. At all costs, I wanted, as Bob Craner often put it, "to hold up my end of the bargain."

My first concern was not that I might fail God and country, although I certainly hoped that I would not. I was afraid to fail my friends. I was afraid to come back from an interrogation and tell them I couldn't hold up as well as they had. However I measured my character before Vietnam no longer mattered. What mattered now was how they measured my character. My self-regard became indivisible from their regard for me. And it will remain so for the rest of my life.

Had I accepted that many of the others had surrendered their dignity voluntarily, had agreed to live with such reproachful self-knowledge, I doubt I would have resisted to the extent that I did, and thus I would probably not have recovered from the shame I felt when I was broken.

This is the truth of war, of honor and courage, that my father and grandfather had passed on to me. But before my war, its meaning was obscure to me, hidden in the peculiar language of men who had gone to war and been changed forever by the experience. So, too, had the Academy, with its inanimate and living memorials to fidelity and valor, tried to reveal this truth to me. But I had interpreted the lesson, as I had interpreted my father's lesson, within the limits of my vanity. I thought glory was the object of war, and all glory was self-glory.

No more. For I have learned the truth: There are greater pursuits than self-seeking. Glory is not a conceit. It is not a decoration for valor. It is not a prize for being the most clever, the strongest, or the boldest. Glory belongs to the act of being constant to something greater than yourself, to a cause, to your principles, to the people on whom you rely, and who rely on you in return. No misfortune, no injury, no humiliation can destroy it.

This is the faith that my commanders affirmed, that my brothers-in-arms encouraged my allegiance to. It was the faith I had unknowingly embraced at the Naval Academy. It was my father's and grandfather's faith. A filthy, crippled, broken man, all I had left of my dignity was the faith of my fathers. It was enough.

*To have courage for whatever comes in life—
everything lies in that.*
—MOTHER TERESA

ICE BOUND

DR. JERRI NIELSEN

Amundsen-Scott South Pole Station, October 16, 1999. Today I take my last snowmobile ride in Antarctica—from the ice-crusted dome where I have lived for eleven months, to the edge of an airfield plowed out of the drifting snow. Normally I could walk the distance in a few minutes, but I am too weak. My best friend, Big John Penney, drives me up the mountain of snow we call Heart Attack Hill to the edge of the flight line. We are bundled in our red parkas and polar boots, extreme-cold-weather gear that weighs nearly twenty pounds. I'm wrapped in so many layers of fleece and down that I can barely move. My hair was long and blond when I arrived at the Pole, but now my head is completely bald, and coddled like an egg in a soft wool hat beneath my hood. I wear goggles and a neck gaiter up to my eyes to keep my skin from freezing. It is nearly sixty degrees below zero.

Big John helps me off the machine and we stand together for a moment, staring into a solid wall of blowing snow. The winds are steady at twenty knots, causing a total whiteout over the station. Incredibly, we can hear the droning engines of a Hercules cargo plane, muffled by the weather but getting louder by the second. It is the first plane to attempt a landing at the South Pole in eight months.

"He'll never make it," says Big John. "He'll have to circle and turn back."

I can't decide if I am frightened or relieved. I am sick and quite possibly dying.

There is no doubt that I have to leave here to get treatment for the cancer growing in my breast. I am the only doctor among forty-one scientists and support staff at this U.S. research station, and I've been worrying about what would happen if I became too frail to care for my patients. Dozens, perhaps hundreds, of people have worked for weeks to organize this extraordinary rescue flight. I feel grateful and humbled and, at the same time, overwhelmed with grief.

In reporting my predicament, some journalists have described the South Pole as "hell on earth." Others refer to my time here as "an ordeal." They would be surprised to know how beautiful Antarctica has seemed to me, with its waves of ice in a hundred shades of blue and white, its black winter sky, its ecstatic wheel of stars. They would never understand how the lights of the dome welcomed me from a distance, or how often I danced and sang and laughed here with my friends.

And how I was not afraid.

Here, in this lonely outpost surrounded by the staggering emptiness of the polar plateau, in a world stripped of useless noise and comforts, I found the most perfect home I have ever known. I do not want to leave.

But now as the sound of the engines grows to a roar and shifts in pitch, I strain to take a last look around. I am hoping for an opening in the storm, as much for me as for the pilot. I want to see the ice plain one more time, and lose myself in its empty horizon. But the notion passes, like waking from a dream, and within moments begins to seem unreal.

Facing it—always facing it—
that's the way to get through. Face it!
—JOSEPH CONRAD

THE BEST ADVICE I EVER HAD

MAURICE CHEVALIER

*L*ife was just about perfect, I told myself, feeling immensely thankful that fate had been so good to me. Truly I was sitting on top of the world. I had been the star of a hit musical revue on the Paris stage for a year. I'd been signed to make four movies at an important studio. Best of all, I had scores of good friends whom I saw often.

That was in 1922. I did not know then how soon all my good luck was to end.

Looking back later on what happened at Les Bougges Parisiens that evening, I realized there had been warning signs. For months I had been working too hard, sleeping too little, and exhaustion occasionally caught up with me—a terrible heaviness of spirit, a draining of morale. I had ignored it, however. "Momentary fatigue," I would say, and move out before the footlights, forcing the gaiety that the audience awaited.

This night, however, was to be different. At a long lunch with friends, I'd foolishly indulged in too much rich food and too many wines. I had taken a nap, expecting to be myself again before curtain time. But at the theater my brain still seemed to be on fire. I had never felt this strange dizziness before, and I tried to dismiss it as I waited for my opening cue. When the cue came, though, the words seemed to reach me from far away. I responded with my customary lines—or so I thought. But something obviously had gone wrong. I could see it in my fellow actor's eyes.

When I answered his second speech, I saw surprise turn to alarm, and I realized with horror that I had replied to both his cues with lines not from the first act but the third! Desperately I tried to get back on track, but my mind was now suddenly a jumble. I was hopelessly lost.

The actor with whom I played the scene covered up for me beautifully, whispering the opening words of each of my lines, as did others in subsequent scenes. Somehow the evening came to an end with only those backstage the wiser.

The rest of the cast laughed off the episode as a temporary upset. I wanted to believe them, but I was badly shaken. What if tonight were only the beginning? An actor who couldn't remember his lines—this could mean the end of a career which had brought me from rundown Montmartre cafés where I had sung for food to the finest theaters in Paris and a salary of thousands of dollars a week.

The next day I went over and over my lines, rehearsing speeches and songs I had known perfectly for a year. But that night the panic returned, and with it a nightmare existence I was destined to suffer for months. Onstage I found myself unable to concentrate on the lines I must say at the moment; instead, my mind would race to those which lay far ahead, trying to ready itself in advance. I hesitated, stammered; the debonair ease that had been my trademark as an entertainer was gone. And then came attacks of vertigo, when the floor would whirl up to meet me in a dizzying spin. I was afraid I might actually fall in the middle of a scene.

I visited one specialist after another. Nervous exhaustion, they said, and tried injections, electric massages, special diets. Nothing worked. People began to gossip openly that my performances were slipping. I tried to avoid my friends, certain that they must be aware that something was wrong.

With pressure building up inside me, a nervous breakdown seemed inevitable. It came. And with it came a conviction that I was really through.

The doctor ordered me to a rest home in Saujon, a tiny village in southwest France. The world of Maurice Chevalier had crumbled, I told myself, and nowhere would the pieces ever be put together again. But I reckoned without the wisdom and gentle patience of the graying, intelligent doctor who was awaiting me in Saujon. With my dossier before him, Dr. Robert Dubois outlined a simple treatment of rest and relaxation.

"It will do no good," I said wearily. "I'm beaten."

But in the weeks that followed I took the long, solitary walks on country roads that Doctor Dubois suggested, and I found a certain peace in the beauty of nature, which has never left me. There came finally a day when Doctor Dubois assured me that the damage to my nervous system had been repaired. I wanted to believe him, but I could not. The inner turmoil did seem to be gone, but I still had no confidence in myself.

Then one afternoon the doctor asked me to entertain a small group at a holiday celebration in the village. At the thought of facing an audience—any audience—I felt the blood drain from my head. I refused abruptly.

"I know you can do it, Maurice," he said, "but you must prove it to yourself. This is a good place to start."

I was terrified. What guarantee would there be that my mind would not go blank again?

"There are no guarantees," Doctor Dubois said slowly. And then he went on with words that I can hear as clearly today as thirty-seven years ago: "Don't be afraid to be afraid."

I was not sure what he meant until he explained.

"You are afraid to step onto a stage again, so you tell yourself you're finished. But fear is never a reason for quitting; it's only an excuse. When a brave man encounters fear, he admits it—and goes on despite it."

He paused, waiting for my reply. There was a long moment before it came. I would try.

I returned to my room trembling at what lay ahead. I spent hours of torture during the next few days going over the words of the songs I would sing. Then came the final trial: when I stood in the wings of the tiny auditorium, waiting to go on.

For an instant, as panic mounted in me, I was tempted to turn and run. But the doctor's words echoed in my ear: *Don't be afraid to be afraid.* And then suddenly the amateur orchestra was playing my cue, and I moved onstage and began to sing.

Each word I sang and spoke that evening was anguish. But not once did my memory play me tricks. When I walked offstage to the sound of enthusiastic applause, I felt a triumphant joy welling up inside. Tonight I had not conquered fear; I had simply admitted it and gone on despite it. And the scheme had worked.

There was a road back after all. Probably I would never quite regain my old assurance, I told myself, for what had happened once could always happen again. But I could live with it now, and I was determined to prove it.

The path to Paris was not easy. I chose to begin it in Melun, only a few miles from the French capital. I selected a small movie theater, located the startled manager and offered to sing for a sum so low he thought I was joking. When I convinced him that he was helping me toward my comeback, he agreed, and I began a pattern that was to take me to city after city for many weeks. Each performance was an agonizing strain.

"So you are afraid," I would whisper to myself every time. "So what?"

I said that same thing when, at last, I waited for my cue in a magnificent new theater in Paris, willing finally to face the challenge of a Parisian appearance. The curtain fell that night on the beginning of a new world for me. Applause shook the theater. I answered calls for encores until I could physically do no more. Success, which I had once had and lost, was mine again.

Since that night, for almost four decades, I have gone on doing the work I love, playing for audiences everywhere. There have been many moments of fear, for the gentle doctor of Saujon was right: There are no guarantees. But being frightened has never again made me want to quit.

How often has fear been the barricade at which we have all halted in our tracks! We can see what we want beyond, but rather than admit we are afraid and go ahead nonetheless, we so frequently invent excuses and turn back in defeat.

But my own experience has taught me this: If we wait for that perfect moment when all is safe and assured, it may never arrive. Mountains may not be climbed, races won, or lasting happiness achieved.

How sublime a thing it is to suffer and be strong.
—HENRY WADSWORTH LONGFELLOW

REAL STRENGTH

CHRIS PENDERGAST

I'd always thought myself to be a decent teacher. I loved my work and threw myself into it. For twenty-three years, I crafted my trade and honed my skills. By age forty-four, I was a seasoned and competent educator. Life, both personal and professional, had developed a rich fullness, like a ripening fruit in the warmth of summer's sun. Then, on a dank, drizzling October eve, a call came from my neurologist, a call that made my world implode. "I am sorry to tell you, but you have ALS." ALS (also known as Lou Gehrig's disease) is a rapidly progressing neuromuscular disease with no known cause, treatment, or cure. It runs its nasty, paralyzing course in an average of a brief two to three years. I was sentenced to die.

The first of many choices I faced was how I wanted to spend the rest of my life. It was not exactly a yes/no question. Quite early, I made my decision. My life was good. I wouldn't change a thing. In spite of the challenges to come, I knew I wanted to continue teaching.

Little did I realize that this darkest hour would produce my brightest moments. As I began to publicly battle ALS, my class, my school, and my district became my allies as I shifted from teacher to learner, from leader to explorer. We all became a team, learning life's important lessons together.

Part of my teaching assignment in the gifted and talented program is the operation of a mini-nature center called the Habitat House. It houses many animal species gathered for children in a living laboratory. Students assume a wide range of animal-care tasks. Lunch periods find my room a veritable beehive of activity. Like worker drones, children incessantly move about tending to their charges. A large magnetic chalkboard ruled off into a grid serves as the master scheduler. It lists a myriad of feeding details including animal names, cage numbers, food types, and amounts. Each animal has a small square magnet occupying the last square of the grid. It is coded with red on one side and green on the other. When a student scans the board for a task to complete, they immediately are directed to which jobs need to be done—they're green. Upon selection of a particular "green" job, the student must turn the magnet to red, signaling "Stop" to other children.

During an orientation session to Habitat House, a timid third grader patiently listened to my detailed procedures. When instructed, she approached the board and viewed her options. Her head rotated as she scanned the list. After an inordinate interval, she turned and looked at me. I labored toward her. She stated in a soft voice, "Mr. P., I need help. I want to feed the iguana but I can't." I bent down to inquire the nature of her problem. I gently probed, "Do you understand the board?" Her head bobbed in affirmation. Perplexed, I searched wider, "And, you know where the supplies are?" Again, she nodded. Her eyes, on level with mine, seemed tense and unsure. Remaining hunched to be close, I finally asked, "Well honey, what is it?"

She raised her hand, index finger extended and pointed to the chalkboard. Her arm was angled up and fixed on the iguana row. "It's too high, I can't reach to turn the magnet. Will you do it for me?" I momentarily froze, helpless, as I sensed my paralyzed arms hanging limply at my side. I seemed unable to help this young girl. She waited with an innocent stare that burned through me. I interpreted her body language as saying, "Well, are you going to help me or not?"

Whenever I faced the decision to continue to teach with severe disabilities, a haunting reality shadowed me. Will I recognize when the time comes that I should retire, when my limitations exceed my contributions?

Sixty-odd years ago, Lou Gehrig faced the same moment of truth. After a historic string of more than two thousand games stretching thirteen years, Lou left baseball. "Leave at the top of your game" is a mantra spoken by all who are challenged by declining performance, and it was certainly one I had wrestled. As I faced this young girl, I seemed on that cusp. I couldn't help her with the simplest request. I was hurting rather than helping. But this sweet, eager young child was about to teach me a lesson in life and about myself.

Intellectually, I always knew teaching was a magical interaction between the teacher and learner. John Dewey, the father of American education, captured it when he told us, "Learning is not a spectator sport." Yet emotionally, I was a prisoner of the need to "always know and to be in charge." ALS reshaped my world and forced me to reassess who and what I was. Now, this girl was doing the same thing.

I searched frantically for a resolution to her quandary. Gently, I asked her if she was aware of my muscle disease. She nervously smiled and whispered, "Yes."

"Well, hon, I can't help you. My arms are too weak. I can't raise them up that far," I confessed. Relieved at my own truthfulness, I nervously awaited her response. I anticipated her selection of a new animal, one that was literally more within her reach. Instead, she continued to just look at me. Her mind was focused; she wanted the iguana.

Suddenly, it came to me. "Hon, I can't solve your problem alone. But, if we work as a team, I think we can solve it together. Your arms are too short, my arms are too weak. If we help each other, we can do it."

I motioned to her to grasp my thin, limp arm. Quite reluctantly, recognizing the unorthodoxy of it all, she took my arm. "Great!" I exclaimed and encouraged her to push my arm up. Stretching on her toes and straining under the weight of my long arm, she inched my hand to the top of the chalkboard, a good six feet high. Her fingers pressed into the flesh of my upper arm and I heard a moan as she made a last effort. Hitting the magnet, my fingers managed to flip it to red. Spent, she let my arm go. It fell and thudded against my leg. Then, she left, content to do her job.

I stood there, the impact of what happened slowly sinking in. I realized I was no longer physically able. I understood I was no longer in charge of circumstance. I understood I couldn't be the solution. I also realized we needed to be a team, a true team united by common goals and purpose. I really learned our strength is in our collective abilities, not our individual weakness. After first hearing Dewey's words, it took me awhile to finally get it—twenty-five years to be exact. Guess I'm a slow learner, but better late than never.

I continue to teach. My muscle deterioration advances. Each day brings a new challenge. It also brings an opportunity to learn and grow. ALS, rather than a death sentence, has become my master teacher.

The virtue of adversity is fortitude,
which in mortals is the heroical virtue.
—FRANCIS BACON

NINTENDO MASTER

KATIE GILL

hen I first saw you, I thought—*Nintendo Master.* There was this intensity about you. Your piercing blue eyes and the way your hands moved rapidly along the control buttons were subtle hints of your expert skill.

You didn't appear too different from all of the other video-crazed ten-year-olds out there, but you were. I guess the fact that it was summer, and we were both stuck in the oncology ward of the hospital cruelly betrayed the normalcy with which you tried to present yourself. Or maybe it was the fact that we were prematurely robbed of the innocence of childhood, and it comforted me to know that there was someone else out there just like me. I can only speculate, but all I know for sure is that I was drawn to your energy and zest for life.

That was the summer of my first post-cancer surgeries. The doctors were trying to fix my left hip joint, which had shattered under the intense bombardments of chemotherapy treatments. It wasn't the only thing that had shattered. I had misplaced my usual optimistic attitude about life and was surprised at how nasty I could be. This did not help me endear myself to anyone.

My surgery went "well," the doctors said, but I was in excruciating pain. (The ever-present differing perspective of doctor and patient is an amazing thing.)

I saw you again in physical therapy, realizing only then the extent of what cancer did to you. I wanted to scream, "Let him go back upstairs and play his video games, you idiots!" But I just sat there in stunned silence. I watched you get up and start walking with the aid of the parallel bars. Prior to your entrance into the room, I sat in my wheelchair wallowing in self-pity. I thought, "Wasn't the cancer enough? Now my hip is screwed up, and I really don't care anymore. If I get up, it is going to kill me."

You will never know me, but you are my hero, Nintendo Master. With such courage and poise, you got up on your one remaining leg. Some might have the audacity to call you disabled or even crippled, but you are more complete than many can ever wish to be. After you had your walk for the day, a walk that was perfectly executed on your part, and you were safely tucked into your bed enjoying your video games once again, I decided that it was about time that I got up and took a walk myself. You see, Nintendo Master, it dawned on me then that you had innately known what it takes most of us a lifetime to grasp—life is like a game, you can't win them all, and yet the game goes on, forcing all to play it. Nintendo Master, you play it better than most!

Persistence is the master virtue. Without it, there is no other.
—AUTHOR UNKNOWN

GOING THE DISTANCE

VIRG JONES

*A*turned off the alarm and struggled to a sitting position. The bed in my Washington, D.C., hotel room was comfortable, but I'd tossed and turned all night. I was a thirty-six-year-old junior banking executive, one thousand miles from my Kansas City home on the first business trip of my life. Alone. I was scheduled to be at my first meeting two hours from now. Certainly not enough time for even a quick therapeutic swim in the hotel pool. In fact it was barely enough time for someone like me to get ready.

Well, here goes. I picked up the phone. I knew what I was about to ask was going to sound very strange. For all I knew they might throw me out of the hotel. But I needed help. Painstakingly, I punched in the numbers for the front desk.

Asking for help. It isn't something that most people like to do. It's something I rarely did myself until I was diagnosed with juvenile rheumatoid arthritis at age thirteen. I landed in the doctor's office after experiencing persistent swelling in my knees, ankles and hands. I was so sore I quit going to basketball practice. I couldn't even swim laps in the local pool.

"So what's the deal?" I asked the doctor. "Is it going to get better soon? Our first game is in two weeks."

"I'm afraid it's not as simple as that, Virg," the doctor said. "This isn't something that just goes away. In fact, rheumatoid arthritis never goes away."

The doctor's words didn't really register. My teenage brain refused to accept such a thing. Arthritis was an old people's disease. It wasn't going to stop me.

Yet the pain and swelling worsened to the point where I couldn't go to school anymore. My hands grew so crabbed that I could barely hold a pencil. I needed crutches just to walk around the house. I tried to will myself well. I prayed. I begged God. Finally my parents decided to send me to a hospital in Hot Springs, Arkansas, that specialized in arthritis treatment.

The doctors prescribed a drug that was supposed to help keep my joints flexible. I had a bad reaction. Drugs that slow the progression of the disease weren't available back then. Neither were artificial joints. They tried leg splints and traction. Still I got worse. Then came the day when I tried to get out of bed and couldn't. The disease had stopped me cold. I'd sworn it wouldn't, but it did. I was sixteen.

My body has failed me, I thought, *but I still have my brain.* I had to keep my mind strong if I was going to maintain a positive attitude. And I was determined to be positive. What else did I have left? The first thing was to finish my education. I'd missed so much school, and it wasn't clear I'd be returning anytime soon.

So I studied. And memorized. And read. I read almost everything my parents and the hospital staff could get me. From James Michener's historical epics to Robert Frost's poetry. Most of all, I loved Ernest Hemingway. For better or worse, Hemingway's characters took risks. They devoured life and the experiences it offered the way I devoured his writing. I read and reread *For Whom the Bell Tolls*, Hemingway's story of an American professor caught up in the Spanish Civil War who puts everything on the line to fight for what he believes in. The book's message only got clearer each time I read it: Don't ever give up.

Still, at night, in the darkness of my room, trapped in a hospital bed with little chance of ever leaving it, hope seemed as far away as my high school gym or swimming pool. It was at those moments I tried to get closer to God, a God without whom I knew this disease would beat me.

One day when I was twenty-one, an orthopedic surgeon came to see me. "I'd like to operate on you," the surgeon said after examining me. "I want to try an experimental procedure. If it works, your legs will be straight and you'll be able to walk again."

I'd been confined to a wheelchair for five years. I'd try anything.

"What if it doesn't work?" I asked.

"What can be worse than how you are now?"

I thought of Hemingway's characters, people who met life on its own terms. "Let's do it," I said.

The procedure involved fusing my knee joints, followed by four months of traction. *What can be worse than how you are now?* I recalled the doctor's question. Well, traction was worse. My legs were in casts and strapped to pulleys for months. But it ended on the day I stood and walked, if only for a few steps. Day by day I kept walking until I walked out of the hospital's front door and went home.

As soon as I could, I started swimming again—one of the few athletic activities within reach of someone as arthritic as I was. It was difficult at first. I couldn't use my legs at all. I was limited to an awkward dog paddle. I had to use a mask and snorkel to breathe. It took me ages to get from one end of the pool to the other. Turning was difficult. Eventually I just swam around the pool's perimeter instead of down the middle. For the first time in years I was exercising, and it felt great. More than great. It felt miraculous.

Those endless days of reading at the hospital paid off. I passed my GED. I took the SAT and ACT college entrance exams and was accepted at nearby Emporia State University. I made friends there, met my wife, Harriett, and graduated in three years with a dual major in accounting and economics. I got a job in banking and started to move up.

Still, I never strayed far from home. I'd made a nice little life for myself in Kansas City. No, I probably wasn't much like those Hemingway characters anymore. I played it safe, grateful for how far God had taken me. Until I realized that if I wanted to advance my career, I needed to get on a plane and travel.

Which gets me back to that morning in Washington, when I called the front desk at the hotel. I was in a strange city in a strange hotel. I knew no one. And my day—indeed, in a sense, my life—would not go forward until I asked someone to come up here and help me, someone I didn't know from Adam. All at once I thought of those Hemingway characters I had read about in my hospital bed. I remembered the closeness to God I felt in the night when hope seemed so far away. Sometimes real strength, real courage, is asking for help, first from God and then from those he picks to help you.

The desk clerk answered. I said, "I know this might sound strange, but I need someone to come up and help me get dressed."

By the time I got back to Kansas City from that first trip, my entire world had expanded, just as it had each time I had dared to try something new in the past. Maybe I wasn't fighting in wars or getting into bullrings the way the heroes of the Hemingway stories I loved did, but I was doing something that to me was every bit as exciting. I was saying yes to the challenges life presented me with and trusting that when I did, God would send me all the help I needed.

I'm sixty-one now and have been retired for nine years, but I still swim. Every morning and evening I dive in the pool I built in my backyard and do laps for an hour or more. I'm not much of a speed swimmer. You could time me with a sundial. But the water is the place where I feel the freest, where time doesn't matter.

One day a few years back, the local chapter of the Arthritis Foundation asked if I would visit some kids newly diagnosed with arthritis.

"What do you do for exercise?" one of them asked.

"I swim," I said. The children looked at me as if I said I could fly. Those looks triggered an idea. Our Arthritis Foundation chapter sponsored an annual 5K run to raise funds for treatment and research. I couldn't run. But I knew another way I could travel five kilometers.

"I'll match the runners," I told the foundation.

I did my usual circular laps in the pool, cutting slowly through the water, one circle after another for four hours, nonstop. And with each lap I felt something you wouldn't ordinarily associate with swimming in circles: I felt free. The way those Hemingway characters wanted to be free. The way God wanted me to be free.

Cast thy burden upon the Lord, and he shall sustain thee.
—PSALM 55:22

A SIGHT THAT GIVES STRENGTH

DAVE AND JAN DRAVECKY

I met Terry several years ago. She was an avid baseball fan and especially loved the San Francisco Giants. She lived in the Bay area and had followed my career and illness with great interest—not only because she adored the Grand Old Game, but because she was battling a terminal case of cancer.

I got her on the phone one day to try to encourage her in the deadly struggle she faced. We talked about our mutual interests and the excitement of major league baseball, as well as the highs and lows of being a Giants fan. In the middle of our conversation, the course of our discussion suddenly changed, and we began talking about her difficult battle against cancer. I don't recall much of what I said, but I remember vividly what she told me. "The one thing that gets me through this as I lie here in my hospital bed," she declared, "is knowing every morning that, if God once more allows me to open my eyes, the first thing I'll see is a picture of Jesus hanging on the wall at the foot of my bed. When I see that picture of Jesus, somehow I get the strength to make it through another day."

For someone who knows that, there's not a whole lot more that can be said. Terry discovered in her pain what all of us should remember every day of our lives: The way to get through the trials and difficulties of life is by looking to Jesus.

But why? Why should this be any help at all? The writer of the book of Hebrews gives us the answer: "Consider him who endured such opposition from sinful men, so that you will not grow weary and lose heart," he wrote (Hebrews 12:3). So let's do that for a moment. Let's "consider him." What is it about Jesus that will help us to keep going and not lose heart when we face trials of whatever sort?

First, it's helpful for me to consider that he himself did not lose heart. Of what use would he be to me in my affliction if, in the midst of his own troubles, he caved? Thank God, he didn't. He wasn't dragged, kicking and screaming, to the cross. He chose it. "I lay down my life—only to take it up again," he said. "No one takes it from me, but I lay it down of my own accord" (John 10:17–18). He never wavered from his course, even when given the opportunity. When Peter tried to thwart his arrest in the Garden of Gethsemane, Jesus commanded him, "Put your sword away! Shall I not drink the cup the Father has given me?" (John 18:11). When the Roman governor Pilate suggested it was up to him whether Jesus lived or died, the Master replied, "You would have no power over me if it were not given to you from above" (John 19:11). Even in his last few excruciating moments on the cross, Jesus showed his unbroken spirit. He forgave those who crucified him. He welcomed a dying thief to his new home in heaven. He arranged for the care of his widowed mother. Jesus never lost heart, even as he left this world with the shout, "Father, into your hands I commit my spirit" (Luke 23:46).

Second, it encourages me to keep going in my trials when I consider how infinitely greater his sufferings were. No one ever knew suffering as Jesus knew it. His physical suffering was horrible enough—read a medical description of what happens during crucifixion sometime, if you can stand it—but many others in history have been put to death in exactly the same way. What made Jesus' death so incomparably worse than any other was that God placed on him—a man who had never known even a moment of sin's contamination—the entire vile volume of the sin of the whole world. "God made him who had no sin to be sin for us, so that in him we might become the righteousness of God," Paul wrote in 2 Corinthians 5:21. As one commentator has written:

"Christ has thus become his people's supreme inspirer of faith. When they become weary on the way, and grow faint at heart because there seems no end to the trials they have to endure, let them consider him. He suffered uncomplainingly the hostility and malevolence of sinful men; the recipients of this epistle [Hebrews] had not been called upon to endure anything like their Master's sufferings."

Martin Luther, the great reformer, would say this even more forcefully. "Our suffering is not worthy the name of suffering," he wrote. "When I consider my crosses, tribulations, and temptations, I shame myself almost to death, thinking what are they in comparison of the sufferings of my blessed Saviour Christ Jesus." And R. C. Sproul joins in the chorus when he says, "No one was ever called by God to greater suffering than that suffering to which God called his only begotten son. Our Savior was a suffering Savior. He went before us into the uncharted land of agony and death." When suffering invades their lives, many complain, "God doesn't understand!" But he does. He understands it far better than we do. Our Savior suffered vastly more than we will ever begin to grasp—and he did it for our sake.

Last, I am helped to endure my trials when I consider how Jesus endured his own: ". . . who for the joy set before him endured the cross" (Hebrews 12:2). Jesus looked ahead to what his sufferings would accomplish, and great joy gripped his soul. He endured for the joy of completing the Father's will for him. He endured for the joy he would feel at his resurrection and exaltation. And he endured for the joy of soon being able to present cleansed believers to the Father in glory. Jesus did not "enjoy" the cross, but he was able to endure it for the joy set before him.

I'm not sure how much of all this Terry understood as she gazed morning after morning at a picture of Jesus hanging on the wall at the foot of her bed, but she obviously understood enough. When she considered Jesus, she took heart and was able to endure. And so can we.

I bend, but I do not break.
—JEAN DE LA FONTAINE

BROUGHT DOWN TO GROUND LEVEL

FRED EPSTEIN, M.D., AND JOSHUA HORWITZ

It's been said, to have children is to give hostages to fortune. All parents live in dread of their child becoming seriously ill, and they pray that it will never happen. When it does, their hearts are ransomed to fear. They have to walk a treacherous tightrope between despair and hope, between terror and courage.

I meet these parents when they come to my office, clutching MRI films in one hand and their sick child in the other. They come from across the country and around the world. During a single week last year, I operated on a Hindu girl from India, a Greek Orthodox boy from Athens, and a seventeen-year-old Buddhist monk-in-training from Tibet. Their parents' responses to their personal crises were as diverse as their backgrounds. And yet, having a sick child tends to erase all cultural difference. Every parent has to face his or her apocalypse from scratch, has to cope with the fear and the anger, has to fight for faith with whatever tools they have.

My own test of faith began with a phone call I got at my office four years ago. It was the Friday of Columbus Day weekend, a busy morning at the Institute for Neurology and Neurosurgery, like most mornings. I was due in the operating room in a few minutes, and a doctor was coming in from out of town that day to interview for a position on our staff.

At the moment, I was on the phone with Jim, the boyfriend of my younger daughter, Ilana. It was like a scene out of a '40s movie. He had called to ask my permission to marry Ilana—but he was having trouble getting to the punch line. For the past five minutes he had been telling me how much Ilana meant to him, how much he loved her, and would always love her. I remember thinking how quaint the whole ritual was, how old-world. It was one of the things I liked best about Jim.

My assistant, Donna, came on the intercom. "It's Samara on line three. From Boston." Samara, my older daughter, was a second-year student at Harvard Business School. Though I spent altogether too much time at the hospital while my kids were growing up, I always stopped what I was doing to take their phone calls. I cut into Jim's monologue, "Jim, if she'll have you, marry her. I'm sure you'll both be very happy. Welcome to the family."

Then I got on the line with Samara. She was trying to keep her voice steady, but she was on the verge of tears. "Daddy, the doctor here found a lump in my neck. In my lymph node."

That was the moment the world stopped for me. The moment when my life as a pediatric neurosurgeon collided head-on with my life as a parent. Everything ground to a sickening, screeching halt.

Samara is a passionate runner, and a week earlier she had called complaining of allergy attacks that left her short of breath. I had prescribed some allergy medication, but when it didn't seem to be working, I had urged her to go the university health services to get it checked out. The doctor who examined her discovered a mass in the lymph nodes in her neck.

"They want me to have a CAT scan," she told me now, her voice beginning to break, "but it's a holiday weekend, so they can't do it until Tuesday."

"Samara, get on a plane today. This afternoon." I struggled to keep my own voice calm, but I could feel the blood racing through my head. "Come home and we'll take care of you."

Donna's voice came on the intercom again. "Fred, they're waiting for you in the OR. Are you ready?"

I had our chief radiologist do Samara's CT scan later that afternoon, but we wouldn't have the biopsy results from her lymph node until Monday. That turned into the longest weekend of my life. As it happened, Ilana and Jim were spending the weekend on Fire Island, where we knew Jim planned to propose. Rather than spoil it for them before we had any hard information, we all decided to hold off telling them anything.

Samara slept in her old room, along with our dog. I barely slept at all. I was left alone with my fears, pacing the house until close to dawn, looking in on Samara every hour or so. I remembered sitting in that same bed with Samara as a child, reading *Sleeping Beauty* aloud to her. Now I was the powerless king who couldn't protect his daughter from the witch's deadly curse, no matter how many spinning wheels he burned or banished.

In spite of my macho surgeon credentials, I had always been a wimp when it came to my own children's accidents and illnesses. Ilana's migraines and Joey's asthma attacks sent me into a panic. Kathy had always been the rock on the home front.

The biopsy results on Monday confirmed my suspicion: Samara had Hodgkin's disease, cancer of the lymph nodes. As a doctor, I knew that we had caught Samara's cancer at an early stage and that with prompt treatment she had a good chance of a full recovery. But for a parent, anytime the odds of a cure for your child are less than one hundred percent, they stink. After I got off the phone with the pathologist, I remember thinking, "This is the test of courage I never wanted to have to pass."

Samara insisted that she wanted to go back to school and be treated in Boston, so I went into crisis-management mode.

I spent the evening on the phone with colleagues at Massachusetts General in Boston, assembling a team of specialists to take care of my daughter. At ten o'clock that night, Ilana returned from Fire Island with an engagement ring and a cat-who-ate-the-canary grin on her face. After we shared the hard news and tears with Ilana, Samara said with her trademark dry humor, "This is great. You get a diamond and I get cancer."

Later that week, Kathy and I flew back to Boston with Samara and met with the oncologist at Massachusetts General. He explained the treatment—five months of chemotherapy, followed by radiation—and the side effects Samara could expect, the same ones I myself had recited to countless parents. When we left the oncologist's office, Samara and Kathy sat down on a bench in the hallway and wept. I'll never forget the sight of them sitting there, holding each other and crying. I never felt so powerless and so afraid.

Kathy and I flew up to Boston every other Friday for Samara's chemo. I flew back on Saturday morning to be with our boys at home while Kathy stayed behind to care for Samara. I went to work and pulled myself together so I could take care of my patients. I fought against the paralysis of depression. I got a lot of support from my extended family at the INN—our staff, patients, and their parents. They brought me food, wrote me letters, gave me hugs. It didn't make the pain go away, but it helped keep hope alive—and without hope there is only fear.

There wasn't anything edifying or ennobling about the pain of watching Samara suffer through her treatment. Every young woman's first anxiety about chemo seems to be, "Will I lose my hair?" I've heard it from hundreds of patients. But when Samara asked me the same question, I went to pieces. I didn't want to go into the room the first day Samara was getting chemo. I didn't want to watch anyone stick a needle into her. I went and I watched, and I'm here to tell you that there wasn't any take-away wisdom from watching her body battle against a deadly disease and its toxic remedies, watching her lose weight and strength, watching her beautiful blond hair fall out in handfuls.

The same year that Samara endured twice-monthly chemo for five months followed by daily radiation for six weeks, she graduated from Harvard Business School and landed a job at a leading financial firm in Manhattan. In the spring she helped Ilana plan her wedding, and in July she walked down the aisle as her maid of honor, her hair in a chic, ultrashort style. Samara's been in remission now for several years, and she has a good prognosis. Hopefully, she's cured.

Despite my horror at what she's been through, I recognize that Samara emerged from her ordeal a more self-confident and mature person. She's mentored other young women with Hodgkin's who have become close friends. She enjoys a renewed feeling of health and physical strength. She's taken up distance running and has competed in two marathons. And as with so many of my young patients, surviving her nightmare has fortified Samara's spirit. It's strengthened her belief in God, while giving her a greater appreciation for the fragility of his creation. For Samara, understanding that the world is an imperfect place—a place where terrible things sometimes happen to good people—has made God more accessible and alive.

Here's how she assesses her life today: "I like the person I am, and am still becoming. The experience of Hodgkin's disease is inseparable from that. I wouldn't wish it on anyone else, but I can't imagine myself any other way."

Regardless of everything I've learned about the resilience of young people, it's been hard for me to trust in Samara's special strengths. As much as I take heart from her vitality, the parent in me continues to suffer. Every time she goes in for her six-month checkup I wince where it still hurts inside, where my heart still hasn't healed.

When a child gets sick, a parent's job description changes radically overnight—and it's a job none of us is trained for, as I found out. I know now, in a way that I had only witnessed before, how desperately every parent of a sick child has to fight for his or her own survival and healing. For parents, as much as for doctors, the challenge is to remain open. Even if it's your child who's fighting for survival, there's a natural tendency to shut down your mind and parts of your emotions—the parts that are hardest to deal with.

Over the years, some of our medical staff who are parents have confided to me the deal they make with God: "I'll devote myself to these sick children if you spare mine." Personally, I'd never been able to enter into that kind of negotiation. I don't believe that God causes children to become sick, or protects them from harm. I believe that he endows us with whatever strength we need to endure adversity. After that we're on our own.

But that didn't keep me from praying for Samara's life. I would have made any deal to save her. I was a father, and my little girl was sick.

Samara's illness brought me to my knees as nothing else has, before or since. When you're down at ground level, you realize that our humanity is measured by our power to love, to feel pain, and to persevere.

Vitality shows not only in the ability to persist,
but in the ability to start over.

—F. SCOTT FITZGERALD

ON MY OWN . . . WITH GOD'S HELP

VIOLA CHISHOLM

What a predicament—fifty-five and out of a job! For years I'd worked in community agencies, and I loved it, always helping people, some way or other. But now budgets had been cut and I'd been let go. Right away I started making applications everywhere, but the story was always the same: "You're overqualified, Mrs. Chisholm," or, worse, "Your experience is excellent, but even though you have a college background, we can't hire you without a degree."

"I've always managed, somehow," I told myself. Since the breakup of my marriage years before, I had brought up four children alone. God always saw to it that I had a paycheck; I never once doubted it came from him.

But I'd never been this old before! Or this discouraged. Me, the optimist who cheered others on. It was always my nature to look on the bright side. In my family, people were always saying things to me like, "Sis, what does it take for you to see the rain? A bucket of water poured over your head?" Now my upbeat nature was being sorely tested in a job market that seemed to value youth above all.

Finally I got a job doing alterations at a dry cleaner's. I'd always enjoyed sewing. When I lived in the housing projects I even taught sewing basics such as putting up a hem or sewing on buttons. Working with needle and thread was a talent I'd always had. I called it a gift from God, but I never thought of it as a way of making a living. This job didn't pay much; I was barely getting by.

"You should start your own dressmaking business, Mommy," my daughter Gwenie said. "The way you can sew, it's a waste to be working for someone else."

I smiled. "That's easy for you to say." She was young, making it on her own, as all my kids were by now. And I had to make it too. I sure didn't want them ever having to take care of me.

"You can do it, Mommy," Venita said. "You've got to have faith in yourself." She was turning my words back on me, words I'd used to encourage her.

"But," I said, "at my age . . . "

Venita was hearing no buts. "I've heard people brag about the work you do for them. Have you ever had one complaint?"

"No . . ." I did do some sewing for friends, a taking-in here or a letting-out there, even an original design now and then. But lately I'd been too tired, my eyes strained after a long day at the cleaner's, and I'd been turning people down.

"They'd come back," Gwenie said, "and bring others. At least think about it. Okay?"

"I'll do better than that—I'll pray about it." My faith had always been strong. Back in Virginia, growing up in a family of ten, there were plenty of times when things were slow in my father's contracting work and no money came in. But my mother always said, "The Lord will make a way for us," and he always did. I guess it was natural for me to have that same reliance on God through my own years of struggle. But now, a business of my own? I had become accustomed to the security of a regular paycheck. Besides, I didn't have enough money saved to get started.

I talked to my other children. Diane said, "You should definitely do it, Mommy." The youngest, Gwenie, said, "I'll help you, Mommy." Venita suggested,

"We can even do pickup-and-delivery service." And my son in Texas, LaRue, whooped long distance, "Go for it, Mom!"

Finally, bravely, I gave notice at the dry cleaner's. "I'm going into business for myself," I said, and even though my voice shook a little, the words sounded great. They wished me well.

Daytimes, caught up in the excitement of making plans, there was no time for doubts. But when night came, my prayers were uncertain. *Lord, what if I don't get enough work?*

We found a discount place to print up fliers, and I designed a professional card: *Vi's Alterations Plus. Come By and See Vi. Custom Clothing, Repairs, Alterations, with a Loving Touch.* That last phrase was my "plus."

I arranged a workroom upstairs in my house, with a large table for cutting out fabric, my sewing machine by the window, all my brightly colored threads neatly arranged along one wall, and a rack for hanging finished garments. I was ready.

June 4, 1983. Opening day. Our fliers had advertised an open house, with a discount for work brought in that day. We were up early; my daughters and their friends blew up balloons and decorated the house inside and out with streamers. It was some festive place! Our minister came to dedicate my new business. We all bowed our heads as he prayed: "Lord, be with Viola in this new venture. Lead, direct, and guide her."

The whole street was alive with activity. Venita and her friends played music and put on skits throughout the day. Our signs fluttered a welcome in the summer breeze.

And the people came! Some brought patterns: "Can you do this? I'm so hard to fit." Some brought a whole wardrobe to alter: "I've gained a ton, and let's face it, I'm never going to lose it."

By nightfall I had work to last for weeks and weeks; my workroom was piled high with patterns and material. As I fell into bed, exhausted but exhilarated, my prayers were heartfelt thanks.

I worked happily day after day, my own boss. As I finished each garment the money came in—and went out again as I paid bills that had been piling up. But that was all right: income and outgo, that's what business is all about.

Only pretty soon it didn't balance out. After the first rush of work, people still came in steadily for quite a while. Then there was a lull, a long one. Again my prayers became shaky. *God, has everyone forgotten me?*

Well, he didn't give me any magic solutions. In fact, there seemed to be no answer at all. It was as if there were just me, all alone, to figure things out as best I could. My faith strained at the seams.

And the bills kept coming, forming an untidy heap on the dining room table. Right on top was a notice I couldn't ignore: the power company threatened to cut off my gas and electric. I'm sure my children wouldn't have let that happen if I had told them, but I was too proud to ask for their help. My prayers that night were frantic: *God, cold weather's coming and I need electricity to run my sewing machine. I know you don't want me to be in darkness. Help me find a way.*

Daylight came, and I remembered what someone said in an agency where I once worked. "When you have a problem, take it to the highest authority."

So, I went straight to the power company, praying all the way!

Lord, lead me to the right person. Help me find the right words. And bless this person, whoever he might be.

My insistence on going past the counter people to the supervisor of the credit department surprised me. I was surprised again when this stern-looking man listened patiently as I told him about my struggle to get my own business going.

"Well, that's fine," he said. "But how are you going to pay your bills?"

"God will open doors," I said in a firm voice that hid my fear.

Inside I was shaking and wondering, *What am I doing talking like this, here?* But something was pushing me to go on. "When you depend on the One I depend on, you know help will come, somehow."

His eyebrows went up; he just looked at me a moment, and smiled. Then we worked out a plan that allowed me to pay a little at a time until I got caught up, and he wished me luck.

Well, before things really got better I had to humble myself to accept help from friends, loans I eventually was able to pay back in full. And I learned that I had to do more than beg God for help. I had to get out and take action. So when I went to meetings I talked to people more, handed out my card. Things like that helped, and for a while business picked up again. Then, another lull.

One day, sitting in my workroom, dejected because it was so neat—the racks nearly empty, only a few small jobs waiting on the table—I began to thumb through my collection of patterns. Lovely gowns, prom dresses, casual wear, some of them my original designs. And beautiful lounging pajamas (an old fad I was trying to revive), the greatest thing for comfort at home. Sorting the scraps from all these garments, I fingered each piece of fabric lovingly: blue silk, brilliant red velvet, lovely garden prints. A thought leapt out of the blue: *God doesn't want you to hide your light under a bushel! Show people what you can do!*

"A fashion show!" I said aloud. "That's what I'll do, put on a fashion show!"

I couldn't wait to get on the phone. I called people I'd sewn for, asking them to model the clothes I'd made for them. After a few responses such as "What? Me, a model?" most everyone agreed it would be fun.

Then I had consultations with my daughter, made more phone calls to find a place where we could have a luncheon at a reasonable price and added just enough to the admission price to cover expenses. Venita, an expert with makeup, eagerly offered to help. A friend who did professional modeling for a department store said, "I can show these ladies how to look like they've come straight out of *Vogue*. They'll be great, Vi."

Meanwhile I was busy scouting out donations for door prizes; that would be a big attraction. A new batch of fliers went out, tons of them, and more than one hundred people came, filling all the tables in the Genesee Inn banquet room.

Behind the curtain some of the models were nervous. "I wouldn't make a fool of myself for anyone but you, Vi." ("You won't, honey, I know!") "What if I trip?" ("You won't. Don't even think about it!") "I sure never thought I'd wear this on stage, in front of all these people. And just look at the size of me!" ("You're beautiful in it. That's the whole idea.")

I wanted to show that anyone could look wonderful with clothes made for her, clothes that fit perfectly. Most fashion shows feature fancy, expensive clothes that ordinary people can't afford and really have no use for. I was showing practical things and emphasizing my personal, loving touch. As a highlight, I brought out three models together, showing how the same design could be adapted for a petite, average, and large woman. The commentary, shared by my daughters and a good friend, stressed getting the most out of a basic wardrobe by carefully coordinating a few good, well-fitted pieces.

The audience loved it; I could tell by the pleased murmurs. My nephew played the piano all through the afternoon and my family sang several numbers—to enthusiastic applause. At the finale, when everyone joined in to sing, "Reach Out and Touch Somebody's Hand," we were all jubilant, especially the now-seasoned models. The bonds of our friendship had been strengthened by our working together; and I was touched—moved to tears by the way so many had come to my aid, freely giving help.

Many people asked then and there about having work done; others called or dropped by later. Word got around, in wider and wider circles, about my careful work and my "loving touch." Once again my sewing machine hummed happily all day and on into the night.

Not that all my problems were solved; they never are when you're in business on your own. But I figure I have God as my partner, and I have faith that everything will work out for good in the end.

Each time I pick up a piece of clothing I pray, "Lord, help me to finish this work and finish it well." And I ask God to bless the person who entrusted this garment to me. Then I ask him to take care of me, and he does! I may not have all that I want, but he sees that I have everything I need.

Did I say I was in business on my own? Well, I guess I should correct myself. On my own, with God's help. There's a mighty big difference!

Triumph often is nearest when defeat seems inescapable.

—AUTHOR UNKNOWN

I'M OKAY

TRISHA MEILI

Mention the Central Park Jogger to virtually any adult in New York City, and to millions across the country, and they'll relive their sense of shock at what happened to her, even fourteen years later. I'm not sure why this is so. In the intervening years, there have unfortunately been innumerable beatings and countless rapes . . . yet my case is remembered while the others are forgotten by all but the victims and their immediate families and friends. Perhaps it is because . . . people shuddered to realize such cruelty exists in our exalted species. Perhaps it is also the randomness of the attack . . . the sense that "there but for the grace of God go I." And perhaps it is because people wanted to affirm that there is a better, higher part in the vast majority of us, and they could display that nobility in their desire to comfort me. That comfort, expressed through prayer, through letters, through gifts, through kindness, played an essential part in my recovery. The love and support I received from so many surely motivated me to keep pushing ahead and moving forward.

For more than ten years I've been looking for a way to turn what was truly horrible into something positive, to use my experience as the basis for inspiration, not pity. As it turned out, the attack, meant to take my life, gave me a deeper life, one richer and more meaningful than it might have been. A newspaper reporter once dubbed me "Lady Courage." I was proud of that description, a recognition that what I was going through wasn't easy; it took hard work to recover, and even today the process continues. It took courage to give up my privacy. I never intended to become famous or an inspiration. I am an ordinary woman who experienced an extraordinary trauma. But as the years passed, I felt compelled to take the risk of stepping out of my privacy. My story is not essentially about violence in the cities nor the success or failure of our criminal justice system. Nor is it about vengeance or hate. Rather it is about the capacity of the human body and spirit to heal.

. . . Events, people, and conditions came together to help me heal. I was not defeated by what happened. That healing continues and will, I hope, for the rest of my life. There is no end to it and that is the beauty of the process—the learning and growing never stop. I've learned that healing is as much a function of the heart as it is of medicine. That in recovery one must push and push to get better, yet balance that drive against a recognition of limits that must be realistically accepted. That you will be amazed by achieving what you and others thought you could never achieve. That it's better to be proud of how far you've come than regret the distance—sometimes unreachable—yet to travel. That care for others generates care in yourself. That when you are your most vulnerable, a relationship of trust with caregivers makes all the difference. That pouring your energy into the present rather than being preoccupied with the past is crucial. That the human spirit is majestic in its ability to comfort and be comforted.

Some early writings on my case reflected that I hadn't yet "reached my peak" and now probably never would. That "I could have been or done so much more." That kind of thinking saddens me. What I've learned over the past fourteen years is that it doesn't matter what I could have been. What matters is who I am right now.

And that is a survivor named Trisha Meili who may still not be able to walk steadily or see without double vision or be able to juggle too many ideas at once in her mind. But I have the capacity to be generous and to love. Rather than take away these attributes, the attack allowed me to find them in myself.

Endurance is one of the most difficult disciplines,
but it is to the one who endures that the final victory comes.
—BUDDHA

THE LESSON

JACKIE JOYNER-KERSEE

For many athletes the word "farewell" might as well have four letters. They see it as the end of their glory days, of their turn in the spotlight, of their very lives. I don't have that attitude. I've always known that my time on top would end someday, that someone would come along and eclipse me. I wanted to prepare myself for it and, to the extent I could control it, start walking away before being pushed aside.

The moment I decided the 1996 Games would be my last Olympics, I started planning the next phase of my life. After the Games ended, aside from selected long-jump competitions and personal appearances on behalf of my sponsors, my calendar would be virtually empty. For the first time since I was ten, the bulk of my time would be spent on something other than running, jumping, and competing.

Suddenly, a world of opportunities was available to me. I wanted to dive into the unfinished work at my foundation, including raising the remaining six million dollars to start the first phase of construction on the youth center in East St. Louis. I also was eager to focus more on my personal life. Since our wedding day, I've been buying baby clothes and stashing them away inside a drawer until Bobby and I started a family. Biologically speaking, it's time. In March 1997, I turned thirty-five. I'm ready emotionally, too. Bobby has been talking about having kids for years, but

I wanted to wait until I could give our children my undivided attention. I know how single-minded I am when I'm training. To raise a child in those circumstances would have been unfair and irresponsible.

The night before the long-jump qualifying in Atlanta, burdened with thoughts of whether I'd be risking grave injury by competing, I went to a women's basketball game between the U.S. and Japan at the Georgia Dome. Tara VanDerveer, coach of the U.S. team, sent me a note, asking me to help her fire up the women at halftime if they weren't playing well. But the Americans amassed a fifteen-point halftime lead and went on to beat the Japanese by the same margin. The Dome was packed, the crowd was enthusiastic, and the U.S. women's team played so spectacularly, it was thrilling to be in the arena. I stopped by the locker room afterward, greeted my old friend Teresa Edwards, who played guard, and wished the rest of the team luck. "You've worked and sweated to get to this point—fifty-eight games without a loss," I reminded the eventual gold medalists. "Just two more to go. It's what you've dreamed about. Go get it."

The episode made me nostalgic. I'd made an almost identical speech to my basketball teammates at Lincoln High when we were undefeated and one game away from the state championship. It also shifted my thoughts briefly to overtures I'd received before the Olympics, from both the about-to-be-established National Basketball Association women's league and its competitor, the newly formed American Basketball League (ABL). Both organizations wanted me to trade in my track spikes for basketball sneakers. It was a tempting notion, particularly since I've always enjoyed blazing new trails, and since the existence of a financially healthy women's pro basketball league would give female athletes so many more options.

Eventually, after the Olympics were over, I would take the ABL up on its offer. But first, I had some unfinished business on the track.

It had been five days between my withdrawing from the heptathlon and leaving the stadium in tears, and my returning for long-jump qualifying. I was hoping to dispense with the preliminary round quickly, without unduly straining my leg, so that I'd be in competitive shape for the finals the day after.

What a relief it was to jump 21 feet, 11¼ inches and make the finals on the first leap. I was on the field for less than thirty minutes. Someone walked up to me as I was putting on my warmup jacket and asked if I'd made it. "Yeah," I said smiling. "Thank God!"

The afternoon of the long-jump finals, I could feel every single eyeball in the place when I walked onto the field at the warmup track. My therapist, Bob Forster, and I tried to rearrange the beige bandage on my right leg to make it more comfortable. Carl Lewis, who'd already won the men's long jump in spectacular fashion on his last attempt, came over and gave me a hug. "Come on," he said. "Now it's your turn." He flashed a thumbs-up signal as he walked off.

Inside the tent, Leroy Burrell was lying on a massage table getting a rubdown. I climbed onto the table beside him and said hello while my therapist began wrapping my ankles. Leroy looked over, saw my right thigh and my ankles and laughed. "Gosh, Jackie," he said. "You're all bandaged up. You look like the walking wounded."

I was pretty worried, so the repartee and good wishes helped calm me. As soon as I got down off the table and tried to jog around, though, my leg went into spasms. I thought the bandage might be too tight. I asked Bob to rewrap it. As he finished, it was time to get on the bus and ride to the stadium. Inside the bus, the other athletes sat on the seats, while I stretched out on the floor. I wanted to keep the leg extended and loose. At the stadium entrance, the officials checked our bags, equipment, and shoes and lined us up to walk onto the track. I took a deep breath. This was it.

Just that week, Kenny Moore had written an essay for *Sports Illustrated* about the Centennial Park bombing. The piece recounted his experiences as a member of the U.S. marathon team during the 1972 Olympics in Munich, where Palestinian terrorists killed several Israeli athletes. He discussed the indomitable athletic spirit and what he called the essential lesson of sports: "Everyone suffers. It's what you do with the suffering that lifts and advances us as a species. . . . Athletes turn pain into performance."

I was certainly suffering now. Not just physically, but emotionally. I so badly wanted this Olympic experience to be joyous. I wanted to give my best performance in front of an American audience on American soil. I was so disappointed, so heartbroken that it wasn't turning out the way I'd envisioned. Here was one last chance—six jumps—to salvage something from these Games.

I instinctively grasped the essential lesson and applied it to my predicament. I didn't care if my leg blew up. I wasn't going to quit on myself because of a hamstring problem. I'd told Bobby that morning, "I won't leave the track on a stretcher like I did in Tokyo in 1991. If I have to shed blood out there, I will; but I'm staying until I take all of my jumps."

When I walked onto the field that night, a thunderous ovation began. I studied the arena for the first time. It was vast, with three tiers of seats. Beneath the darkened sky, thousands of camera flashes illuminated the stadium like so many twinkling stars. The crowd of eighty thousand was standing and cheering for me now. I couldn't stop smiling as I looked and listened. My heart was pumping. A flood of adrenaline shot up from my toes to my fingertips. It gave me goose bumps. The affection from the crowd flowed into my pores and turned to pure energy. I felt courageous. I wanted to get out there and give it my all because I knew they were on my side. They were pulling for me as hard as I was pulling for myself. It was the most invigorating experience I've ever had on the athletic field.

I loosened up on the runway after putting on my spikes. After locating the spot I wanted to start from on the runway, I nailed my marker into the ground next to it. The painful throbbing in my leg matched, beat for beat, the pleasant pounding in my chest. I sat down and banged on the bandage with my hammer, trying to beat the spasms into submission and loosen up the tightening muscle. I mixed some Powerade and water together and took a few sips. Then I dipped two fingers into a jar of Icy Hot and tried to slide some of the ointment under the bandage to keep the leg warm. I got up, walked around, and shook the leg out, blocking out the feeling of desperation creeping up on me.

The first jump was terrible. I don't know how far I went, but it was nowhere near long enough. *It's going to be a long night,* I thought. Then I caught myself. *Don't get down on yourself. You have six jumps. If it means you're going to have to slowly work your way through it, then that's what you'll do. Let's just take it one jump at a time.*

After the third jump, I was in sixth place at 22 feet, 6¼ inches. Three tries left.

The fourth jump felt pretty good and I was hopeful, until I saw the line judge raise the red flag signaling a foul. I don't know what happened on the fifth jump. When I landed and got up, all I could do to keep from being frustrated was to laugh. It was pathetic. *Come on, Jackie!* I said to myself, trying to shake things up. *Is that all you have to show the world?*

I walked over to the fence to get some guidance from Bobby before the last jump. He was way up in the stands and had to walk down to a tiny railing that was still a long way from me. We had to shout to hear each other.

"Is it too fast?" I asked.

"Yeah, slow it down. Build in the middle and accelerate at the end," he said.

He turned and climbed the long flight back to his seat. I was struck by how calm he was. Not a trace of excitement or panic. Al was sitting near the railing where Bobby spoke to me. He held his breath each time I stood on the runway, terrified that my leg would blow up at any minute. Mr. Fennoy sat in one of the four far corners, in what would be the end zone in a football stadium. He'd been clocking my runs with a stopwatch to monitor my timing down the runway. But he put it away to watch the final attempt.

As I walked toward my marker, I was oblivious to the crowd's gathering roar, the flashbulbs going off all around me, the camera lenses pointed in my direction, the thousands of live eyeballs and the countless millions of others staring at me through TV screens.

I saw only the strip of Mondo in front of me and the pit of sand beyond it. All I heard was the conversation I was having with my soul. *Well, Jackie. This is your last jump in the Olympics. The ultimate test of everything you believe athletics is about. You have to bear down and focus on the execution. The pain is going to come, but you have to block it out and persevere. Here's where you show them your character and your heart.*

I tapped my right foot behind me and whispered, "Come on Jackie." I gathered my hands, put my legs in motion to run. I was racing down the runway, bringing my knees up. As I prepared for the last four strides, I told myself, "If this leg pulls, then it just pulls!" I attacked those last four steps, planted my right foot and launched. I tried to hold myself in the air as long as I could.

For the first time in my career, when I landed in the pit I didn't know if the jump was good enough. The judge at the foul line raised a white flag, signaling it was fair. Then, the electronic scoreboard flashed 22 feet, 11¾ inches. I had leaped into third place and a spot on the medal stand.

I had to wait a few moments for the rest of the competitors to take their final jumps. But I thought my leap would hold up because the three athletes who were also vying for third place each looked at me wearily after my jump as if to say, "I can't believe you jumped that far!"

When the final results were posted on the scoreboard, the crowd went nuts. I was so overcome with emotion, I wanted to personally thank each person in the stadium. I was so grateful for their support. I went over to Al and hugged him. He was elated, simultaneously laughing and crying. Then, as we left the track, the line of athletes swung past Mr. Fennoy's section and I ran to his open arms and hugged him. I looked at him just the way I had after finishing near the back in my first race as an eleven-year-old, and said the same thing I had that day.

"I tried."

He clutched my head in his hands, pressed my forehead to his and said, "As far as I'm concerned, that was a gold medal performance."

I felt the same sentiment from the cheering fans as I walked around the stadium. They were treating me like a record-breaker and a world-beater, even though I was neither, simply because they knew how hard I'd tried. So many times in my career I'd been made to feel that because I didn't win and didn't win big, nothing I did mattered. But this time, every inch of it mattered. This time, third best was just fine. Those ovations that night in Atlanta fulfilled and satisfied me more than any others I ever had. I left the stadium waving to the crowd, with tears streaming down my cheeks. Bobby was waiting at the edge of the track, as always. We hugged for a long time.

"That was the most courageous thing you've ever done," he said. "I know you were in pain, but you didn't give up. This is a medal to be proud of."

I was proud. As the bronze medalist, I led the procession to the awards stand.

When the medal was placed around my neck, I felt I'd received the highest honor of the competition.

While the national anthem of Nigeria played in honor of the gold medalist, Chioma Ajunwa, I realized that the essential lesson of athletics has also been the essential lesson of my life. The strength for that sixth jump came from my assorted heartbreaks over the years—the loss of my mother, the disappointing performances, the unfounded accusations, the slights, the insults, and the injuries. I'd collected all my pains and turned them into one mighty performance. And I had, indeed, been uplifted by the result. I showed the world that the little girl from East St. Louis had made something of herself. She was a woman, an athlete, with character, heart, and courage.

I shall forever cherish my beautiful bronze medal from the 1996 Games. It is my reward for having learned the essential lesson and passing the tough test. It had been a most joyous Olympic experience after all.

The Courage to Make a Difference

*The greatest good you can do for another
is not just to share your riches, but to reveal to him his own.*

—BENJAMIN DISRAELI

THE LOVING ARMS OF GOD

MARION BOND WEST

For the first time in my life I didn't care about anyone else in the world except my husband, Jerry. And myself. Usually I welcomed the opportunity to become involved in someone's life. But not now.

I eased the car into the special section marked "Radiation Therapy." The hospital let radiation patients park free. Despite the cold November air, we walked slowly because Jerry couldn't walk fast. Inside the familiar waiting room we sat in green leather chairs with others awaiting their daily dose of cobalt. We met there each day, the same people, almost as if we were waiting our turns in a beauty shop or some other normal place.

Jerry always entered the waiting room smiling and made it a point to speak to each person. Inevitably he started a conversation. I'd bought him a warm fur hat since he was bald from the brain surgery that had only partially removed the menacing tumor. Already his memory failed sometimes, and he forgot to remove his hat in the waiting room. I removed it for him, and he didn't seem to mind.

It had been more than two months since that day in September when the first horrendous symptom came crashing down on Jerry. Two massive seizures. I told myself that by now I should have become adjusted to the idea that my husband of twenty-five years was walking around with a malignant brain tumor.

But I hadn't. The "adjustment" simply would not come. Hundreds of times I tried to adjust. I tried mentally picturing myself standing in the ocean. It was an actual scene from my childhood, the time a giant wave had caught me suddenly from behind and flung me around and around like a towel in a washing machine. That day in the sea my feet had touched solid ground at last, but now, in the vivid picture in my mind, as soon as I stood, another giant wave came and then another. They continued to knock me down. They meant to destroy me. I couldn't stand or breathe and I didn't see how I ever would again. Not ever.

Across the waiting room Jerry sat with two other men. His rich, spontaneous laughter brought me back to reality. Now the man sitting by Jerry was laughing, too. The third man leaned way over to join in their conversation. I almost resented Jerry's ability to still be sociable and fun. He never stopped smiling or trying to encourage others. I sat frozen like a store mannequin, staring straight ahead.

"Mr. West," came the familiar soft tone of the nurse's voice calling him over the intercom to the treatment room. I watched carefully to see if he needed my help to get up. No, he was managing alone today. An elderly woman across the room smiled at me. I glanced away, pretending not to see. You're old, I thought with resentment. *All the people here are old. We aren't. We're just in our forties.* The waves came crashing in on me mentally, and I couldn't stand or get my breath. I was under the water again, thinking, *All I want in life is to grow old with Jerry. That's all I want.*

I was staring at the beige wall, determined not to let anyone catch my attention or start a conversation, when God spoke to me. It seemed I hadn't heard from him in so long. God and I used to have daily conversations. Exact words came to me from him. Silently, but clearly. And I loved to speak to him, too. But since Jerry's surgery and the grim-faced doctor's report, I hadn't listened for God's gentle voice.

And my words to him seemed stilted, as if we weren't friends anymore. I never stopped hurting or fighting off fear. And God wasn't saying anything. But today, he was speaking. The message from him came again, loud and clear, and as distinct as the nurse calling Jerry over the intercom.

I want you to go to the woman in the hall and speak to her about me. She's in a wheelchair. You'll know her. . . . You can see her from where you're sitting. Tell her about me and that I love her.

There were several women in wheelchairs, but I knew the one. Frail, she had probably been beautiful once. She clutched the sides of the wheelchair with open apprehension. Most of her hair was gone. She had that gaunt, hopeless look. Her bright pink robe didn't do much to make her look cheerful.

"I don't want to," I told God. "I don't care about her. She's old and I just don't care. What about Jerry and me?"

Obey me. I know what's best for you. Go over now and talk to her.

"She's not going to respond. Look at her. She doesn't care, either. Neither of us cares about anyone anymore."

Go on, Marion.

It was one of the most difficult things I'd ever done, and I'd done some almost impossible things in the last two months. I bent over and spoke softly, "Hello. My name's Marion. What's yours?"

She stared ahead, as though I weren't there.

Keep trying, the silent voice urged.

I touched her hand. I wasn't in any mood to make small talk. "God loves you."

Very slowly her cold blue eyes met mine. She turned her head slightly. She spoke softly, too. "I don't believe in God."

I wasn't surprised, but something stirred within me. I was beginning to care about her. Just a little. It felt good. "That doesn't keep him from loving you. God loves you very much. What's your name?"

She moistened her lips with her tongue. It was an effort. "Thelma. I'm dying, you know. I've never believed in God or asked him for anything, and I won't start now. I'm a stubborn old woman."

"I like you," I said and almost smiled.

"Why?" she gasped.

"Because you're honest. I'll see you tomorrow. Okay?"

She nodded.

Jerry came out of the treatment room, walking that unsteady, confused walk that direct radiation to the brain always caused. I placed the fur hat on him, held his arm, and we left. It always felt good to leave. He was smiling, as always.

I moved about the house in my robotlike fashion, still trying to imagine standing up as the giant waves washed over me. I couldn't stand against such destruction. It was impossible. No one could. But still I tried to picture it in my mind. The idea was so real to me, and I wondered what it would be like, to be able to stand in those waves.

Finally, it was time to go to bed. It was the only time that my mind rested from the agony of Jerry's illness. Mercifully, I could sleep and it was a welcome relief. Jerry was already asleep beside me. I'd halfway been trying to think of something I could take to Thelma. A way of saying that God cared about her. Something she could hold on to and take back to her hospital room. I knew by her bracelet that she was a patient in the hospital. I thought of taking her a Bible, or a statue of praying hands. God interrupted my thoughts: *No, no, no. You don't take something like that to some-one who doesn't even believe in me.*

He was right, of course. I was still debating about backing out of this thing with Thelma. She certainly wasn't encouraging our friendship.

The instructions came quickly: *Look up in the top of your closet, way back in the left-hand corner under some stuff. Get the beautiful, handmade shawl, the ivory one. Give that to Thelma and say, "This isn't a shawl. It looks like a shawl, but it's not. It's the arms of God, loving you." Tell her it's from me. Then wrap the shawl around her with your arms and hug her, a little longer than necessary.*

You'd have to know the kind of closet I have to really appreciate the instructions about the shawl. I hadn't seen the shawl in several months. Messy closets have never bothered me, and Jerry seemed to understand and tolerate my side of the closet. I didn't turn on the light, just tiptoed to the closet and reached up on the shelf, way in the back, left-hand side, under some stuff. My hand went right to the soft, luxurious material and I pulled it out with amazement. God and I were really talking again!

The next morning we arrived for Jerry's cobalt at ten sharp. I looked in the hall at the patients lined up awaiting treatment. Would Thelma really be there? She could come anytime during the day. But there she was in the bright pink robe. I got Jerry seated, removed his hat and hurried over to Thelma. "I have something for you."

"I'm not going to take it. Why should I?" she snapped. "I don't know you."

Standing behind her I pulled the shawl from the bag and carefully placed it around her frail shoulders. I did it slowly and deliberately, and enfolded her in my arms . . . a little longer than necessary. "It's not from me. It's from God. Now it may look like a shawl, but it's not."

I waited a moment. She bit instantly. "Well, what is it then?" Already she was stroking it as one would a kitten.

"It's the arms of God, holding you and loving you."

I came around to the front of her wheelchair. She stared at me, her mouth a small, round O. I seized the unguarded moment. "Thelma, he loves you so much. Receive his love. Receive him. Let him into your heart and life now. Trust him."

"But I've been so stubborn . . . for so long."

"Doesn't matter. he sent you the shawl."

"Could you tell me how to—"

Right in the middle of that sentence an orderly pushed her back to her room. She looked over her shoulder at me and mouthed a thank you. I wanted to run after her, but Jerry was coming out of cobalt, walking very unstably and looking for me.

The weeks crept by. Each day the same. The agony never left. We continued with the radiation treatments, but didn't see Thelma again. Waiting each day, I wanted to see her. It would take only a few minutes to run up to her floor. Jerry offered to go with me. I knew the floor so well. Even where her room was. I could see the floor in my mind. Smell it. Hear the sounds. But I could not go back on that floor. Not yet. Jerry had been hospitalized there several times. The long, shiny hall didn't hold good memories for me. I couldn't even face the ride on the all-too-familiar elevator.

I needed to hear from Thelma. I knew that one of my dear friends worked on Thelma's floor. In fact I found out that she was caring for Thelma daily. I learned that Thelma had been far from a model patient, but one day she showed up on the floor wearing a beautiful shawl and insisting that it wasn't a shawl at all . . . but the loving arms of God. And that he loved her! She told her family and strangers about God's love. Thelma insisted that some strange woman had given her the shawl. I thought that perhaps people were beginning to think Thelma was strange, but from what I knew about her, it didn't bother Thelma what people thought. The reports were that she was never without the shawl.

I sent her a copy of a book I had written. Inside I wrote: "Stubborn old women are God's specialty. He loves you. So do I." An avid reader, she devoured the book in a few hours. She began greeting people. Even smiling. Though she became worse physically, her attitude brightened daily. "As sick as she is," my nurse friend said, "Thelma's eyes have a new sparkle."

Little bits of new faith laced with joy insisted upon taking residence in my heavy heart when I thought about Thelma. She reminded me of the absolute truth of Luke 6:38: "Give and it will be given to you; good measure, pressed down, shaken together, running over, they will pour into your lap. For whatever measure you deal out to others, it will be dealt to you in return."

To me it simply meant that whatever you need desperately, you must give away. It sounds foolish, but it works, even if your husband has a malignant brain tumor. If you need money, you give it away. If you need love, you give that away. And in my case I needed tremendous faith, so I had to give away what little I had.

God began pouring the faith back into me in an unmistakable way. I saw myself back in that ocean scene knocked over by giant waves. I was under the water, struggling, unable to breathe. But the scene changed in an amazing way.

I was standing. The waves were pounding me viciously, shaking me, trying to knock me down again and again. But I stood like a small rock, almost without effort. And I knew that if I'd never obeyed God and reached out to unlikely Thelma, then I might never have stood in the ocean vision or in real life. But I knew for certain now, from seeing myself stand with those giant waves washing over me, that I was going to stand no matter what came against me. Not in my strength, of course. I had none left. But in God's.

Thelma died in January, wrapped in the soft shawl . . . and in the arms of the God she had come to know. She learned a lot about how to give out of her need in the short time she had left. My friend who nursed her told me that Thelma decided to leave her sparkling blue eyes to a blind person . . . someone she'd never met.

Change your thoughts and you change your world.
—NORMAN VINCENT PEALE

TIMID SOULS

THIRZA PEEVEY

I gently turned the knob and pushed open the door to my guest bedroom. Mom was awake. She was perched on the edge of the bed in a white T-shirt nightie, looking terribly frail. Although it had once fit, the gown was miles too big on her now. Her hair straggled across her too-pale face. Dark circles rimmed her eyes. She bravely smiled at me, but I could see the pain in her eyes.

"Do you need anything?" I asked. "It's almost time for your medicine. That should ease things a bit."

She nodded. "Maybe a drink of water."

Her voice was weak and tired. I hated to see her that way, but I was grateful that I could take care of her and grateful that we finally knew what was wrong. At first, the doctors weren't sure what was causing her terrible pain and fluid in her chest around her lung. Then my own doctor diagnosed a return of her cancer. He sent her to a major cancer hospital for treatment. They couldn't find the cancer, and were convinced that his diagnosis was incorrect. Finally, after a tense week, they found a rare form of cancer on the lining of her chest next to her lung. Twenty years after her first bout with breast cancer, the cancer had come back in a different place.

She'd had her first surgery that morning, outpatient. I thought she was too sick to be sent home with me, and I didn't feel capable of taking care of her. It wasn't that she needed much at that stage; I just felt incompetent. I wished I could find some-one else to do it, then I felt guilty for not wanting to care for the mother who had spent her life caring for me.

My mother and I are timid souls. Neither of us has ever had much faith in our talents. Perhaps it is just our personalities. Perhaps it was our upbringing. Maybe it's a bad habit. For whatever reason, we both spent the first half of our adult life look-ing for someone who could do things better than we could: someone to turn to when we got outside our comfort zone.

"Mom, why don't you drive up and meet us? We can start the trip earlier that way, and we won't be tired from driving down to get you the night before," I'd suggest.

"I don't know. You know how I hate to drive," she'd hedge. "I'm afraid I'll get lost and won't know what to do."

"If only I could find a really good trainer who could take this horse and make something of him." I would tell her, after taking someone else's rejected horse and making it into a useful animal. "I'm just not very good at this."

"I wish I could find someone who could really do the music for the church," she would say, after practicing flawlessly all week.

It didn't seem to matter that no one else ever turned up who could do our jobs better. We just assumed we weren't looking hard enough.

Fear is an insidious thing. It wraps its tendrils tightly around you and renders you helpless. It can destroy your ability to enjoy life or to feel confident to take on anything new. Over and over, those little negative voices keep telling you, "Boy, you sure messed that up! What made you think you could do that? It's going to take two or three good people to fix what you messed up." Soon you are burying your talents, like the servant in the Bible, when the truth is, you probably did a pretty good job of it. That is the way life was for Mom and me.

Throughout my adolescence, I watched Mom build walls around herself. Those porous walls let criticism in, but they didn't let it back out. She would replay one harsh comment until she had it memorized, letting an unkind word convince her that she was incompetent.

Comments from my father and grandfather in an age when women were considered second to men convinced my mother that her intelligence was second-rate. "You'd better find a good husband to take care of the finances," Grandpa would tell her. So she became convinced that she wasn't capable of balancing a checkbook.

When Grandpa taught my mother to drive, his constant shouting, "Did you see that car?" convinced her that she could never be a safe driver. When her high school art teacher commented "You have no artistic ability," Mom believed that, too. Although that leaves her the only person in the family who doesn't paint or draw, and she has a wonderful decorating sense, she remains convinced to this day. Her piano teacher, likewise, convinced her that she had no musical talent, even though she has nearly perfect pitch and a wonderful voice.

She was a wonderful, creative kindergarten teacher who taught kids to read and write by giving them something to read and write about. She would start with a trip to an orchard to show them how apples were grown and picked. Then she would cook apples and make applesauce in class. They would read every storybook about apples that she could find. Finally they would write about their experiences with apples. This is standard practice now, but in the early seventies she was far ahead of her time.

Unfortunately, those ahead of their time often get criticism from those who are behind the times. She let that criticism eat away at her until she believed that she was a bad teacher, although the responses she got from her former students and their parents every time we saw one in a shopping center should have told her otherwise. "Look, Mom, its Mrs. Charles," they would squeal, dragging their parents off their feet as they came running to wrap my mother in a big bear hug. "I remember when she took us to the orchard," they would invariably say. Sometimes it would be some other little activity that they would recall, or comfort for a childhood scrape. I was often jealous of how much they loved her.

Eventually, she retreated to the life of a farm/house wife. She excelled on the farm, baking all our bread, growing a huge garden, canning and freezing all our food, patching jeans, and darning socks. I suppose she was happy doing it, as she didn't want to leave it. For eight years, she stayed home on the farm, venturing out only to go to church or to pick up supplies if she could find someone to drive her. My mother and I have been close all my life. She was quite young when I was born and I was her only child. Quite serious-minded and protective, I sometimes mothered her as much as she mothered me. We joked that we raised each other. I learned to take care of many of the things that she feared, driving her where she wanted to go, taking care of carpentry and mechanical tasks, bolstering her confidence.

The funny thing is, I learned to be afraid of the things she handled confidently. Where she feared meeting new people, I would talk to anyone, but where she formed close lasting relationships, I withdrew. Where I learned to fix almost anything, she wouldn't touch tools, but where she would take a risk to buy a farm or build a house, I lived in apartments to minimize my financial risks. Where I would take on a twelve-hundred-pound animal, she stayed in the house, but where she would tackle a professional position, I cowered and took minimum wage jobs. We had become almost two half-people who together made a whole.

Now I was facing the prospect of losing her. Although I was married, and a bit more independent, the thought of losing her struck terror in my heart. Even though I could take care of myself, I didn't know what I would do without her. All of my life she had been my rock, my best friend, my comfort in times of trouble. Almost as terrifying was the thought that I would be the one to take care of her. I just didn't know how to do it.

The surgery that morning had gone well, but the recovery room was pretty bad. I stood in the middle of what seemed to be Grand Central Station as patients were wheeled in and out on gurneys. Everywhere around me, people were shouting, "Can you hear me, Mrs. _____? You are in the recovery room." Or "Don't cough, you'll make yourself bleed. It's just from the tube that was down your throat. Can I get you some ice?" Monitors beeped. Carts rattled. Sneakers squeaked across the slick linoleum floors.

I held Mom's cold hand and watched this beehive of activity. The nurse had fetched me from the waiting room when Mom first stirred and asked for me. By the time I got there, she had fallen back asleep. "Just have a seat there, she'll wake up again in a minute," the nurse directed. Then she disappeared.

I sat gingerly in the chair by Mom's gurney, feeling decidedly out of place. Machines beeped and whirred and I had no idea what they meant. With the nurse gone, I had no one to ask. All the noise and movement was bewildering. I was definitely out of my comfort zone here. A few moments later, Mom grunted and stirred. Her eyes flew open and she looked into mine. "Cold," she whimpered.

I looked around for a nurse to take care of her needs. I certainly couldn't help her myself. What did they expect of me? I needed someone more competent. Where were they when you needed them? People scurried around the room at a breakneck pace. Mom's nurse was nowhere to be seen. I didn't know where to get a blanket. "Lord," I prayed silently, "I don't know how to handle this. Show me."

I thought back to when Mom was my age. Getting up to go to the bathroom late one night, I found Mom in her big blue armchair. "What are you doing up?" I asked.

"Praying and reading my Bible," she answered.

I shook my head and padded back to bed. If she wanted to stay up half the night, that was her business. I was going to get some sleep.

The next night, I found her there again. This wasn't like my mother. She wasn't particularly religious. For years, she disliked churches and stayed away from them. Now that she was attending church, she always seemed to hold faith at arm's length. It wasn't like her to give up sleep to pray.

"What are you doing this for?" I asked curiously.

"I am tired of being afraid all the time," she said. "I have been scared all my life. The Bible says that the spirit our God gives us is not a spirit of fear. Fear doesn't come from God, and I don't want it. I'm going to pray and claim that promise until I am not afraid anymore."

I didn't quite believe what I was hearing. Yet, she stuck with it, and over time I started to see a change. Over the next months, she began to stand up for herself more. By the time I left home, she began to drive again. Within a year, she took her first job in eight years, as a cook in a local grocery store deli.

She didn't stop there, either. After less than a year in the deli, she took a part-time job in the local junior college library. After a year, she became full-time. When Barbara, the head of the developmental education department, found out Mom had a teaching certificate, she requested that Mom be given leave time to teach a few remedial reading classes. Soon Mom was working on a master's degree and teaching full time. Mom later became Director of Academic Support.

Sitting by Mom's bed in the recovery room I realized that, with her example before me, I had to follow suit. "Lord," I prayed, "I don't know how to take care of Mom and I'm scared. I know that fear doesn't come from you. Please help me to ignore it and do my job here. I am her daughter and I have a duty of love to take care of her. Show me the way."

Abruptly Mom whispered, "Sick!"

"Are you going to throw up?" I asked.

She nodded vigorously. Where was that nurse? I wasn't equipped to handle this.

Suddenly Mom was sick all over the blankets. I spied a basin on a nearby cart and grabbed it. I held the basin and her head until it was over. Then I pulled the blanket away from her and used a clean corner to clean her up as best I could. I rolled up the blanket and put it out of the way. Then I pulled the others up and tucked them around her. I began rubbing her hands and arms to warm her. When the nurse came, I got more blankets and a wet washcloth. For the next couple of hours, I kept things under control so that the nurses only had to bring me supplies and check the monitors.

"We wish every patient had someone to look after them like this. It makes our job easier," they joked.

"Well, she is my mother," I said, marveling that anyone could think I was doing a good job.

"Most patients don't have anyone to help them the way you are," one nurse confided.

Their words gave me a glow of confidence. Maybe I could handle this.

I tended Mom for the next couple of hours. With each passing crisis I gained more confidence. Each time she asked, I supported her and held the basin.

After she was released from the hospital, I settled her into my guest room and tended to her every need. I checked on her constantly and woke her every four hours for medicine. She stayed with us several days until she could take care of herself.

Two months later, she underwent a second surgery. This time she was in the critical care unit for eleven days, as they did surgery to seal her lungs so that fluid would no longer pool around them. The surgery was painful and draining. Afterward, she had no appetite for days. The nurses sent for the nutritionist to see what they could feed her that she actually wanted. Nothing they offered tempted her. So I went to the farmer's market and brought home fresh vegetables to cook for her.

By the end of the week, she finally began to eat enough for them to send her home to me. That was when we finally figured out what she wanted. Within an hour of walking in our front door, she ate three whole tomatoes. I kept the supply stocked and within three days she was strong enough to go home.

Nowadays, Mom is well and strong again. Her doctors say that as long as she continues to take her medication, she likely will die of old age rather than cancer. They give her twenty to thirty years. I thank God daily for the gift of time with her, time that I almost didn't get. While I am at it, I thank him for showing me that he didn't leave me bereft of competence or talent and for helping me overcome my fears. The act of overcoming those fears left me stronger than I ever had been. Better yet, it strengthened the bond between my mother and me. I can't think of a greater gift.

We can do no great things, only small things with great love.
—MOTHER TERESA

DOING SMALL THINGS WITH GREAT LOVE

MARY ALICE SCOTT

My high school yearbook sold advertisements each year to parents of graduating seniors to print inspirational quotes and congratulatory messages for their children. My mom bought one. She put a picture of me as a little kid, looking silly, with spaghetti on my head or something and a little note that said "Congratulations"—pretty typical. But at the bottom was this quote from Mother Teresa: "We can never do great things, only small things with great love." I don't think I ever told my mom how much that affected me. I'd gone through high school determined to do great things, just because they were great. It never occurred to me to do things out of love.

I did have a sense of responsibility to make changes in the world, but that came more out of my guilt in my own life situation—upper-middle-class, intellectual, athletic—than out of a love for the world or even my own community. I flew off to college and enrolled myself in as many social activist groups as I could find and decided that I was an atheist. I honestly don't know what connection that had with anything. I just decided it one day, literally. I remember the day I decided. I was sitting in my room, not feeling particularly depressed or happy, not stressed or relaxed, just kind of sitting. I looked out the window and didn't see anything—I mean, I saw the sun and the sky and people sitting outside, playing Frisbee, but I didn't really see anything. And so I thought that if I couldn't see anything, then there must be no God. It was a completely unemotional decision.

Of course, looking back now, I think that decision was what put me in a place to find grace. I didn't expect anything. I didn't know at the time what I was being prepared for. I just felt frustrated with my life in general and couldn't quite put my finger on the cause.

In college, I enrolled in the secondary education program, deciding that I would change the world through teaching. Somehow, instead of working in a high school history class, I ended up teaching writing to a small group of fourth graders. That was OK with me. I just wanted to teach.

I walked into the school on the first day and was introduced to my students—Kevia, Cheyenne, Demarcus, and Shawn. Kevia immediately attached herself to me, dragging me into the room in which we would be working together for three hours a week for about four months. My task was to work with these four students on writing exercises so that they could pass the end-of-year writing test and move on to the fifth grade. I pulled out the first writing assignment given to me by the teaching assistant in my education class.

"Start by inciting their imagination. Writing should be fun, not a chore."

I agreed with that. I'd written in a journal since I was nine and loved every minute of it.

"Ask the students to think about a time in their lives when they were the happiest. Have them write about the scene in which they find themselves. You might start by exploring what the scene of a story is."

Great! I could do that. I began by talking with them about what a scene is. It was going well. They got it. Then I asked them to think about a time in their lives when they were the happiest. They screwed up their faces, doodled on their paper, asked each other, and came up with nothing.

"My mom's in jail right now, but it's not right. She shouldn't be there. That doesn't make me happy," one student said.

"Yeah, my dad's girlfriend is pregnant, and my mom's mad, and all she does is cry."

"I don't want to write."

"Yeah, me neither."

What was I supposed to do with this?

"OK, let's write instead about hard times in our lives. Can you describe that scene?"

What was I thinking? I just didn't know what to do. I was so shocked by the responses I got that my brain just wasn't working. Shawn began writing. Thank goodness. The others saw him, picked up their pencils, and bent their heads over the papers, working slowly, methodically forming each letter. I relaxed. I thought that Shawn must have picked up on my inability to connect with them and was trying to help me out.

About ten minutes later, Shawn showed me his work. I couldn't read it. It wasn't that it was messy. In fact, the letters were very neatly formed; they just weren't letters from the alphabet I knew. He didn't know how to write. The other kids passed in their papers. All the same. Every once in a while on each paper there were a few letters I recognized, but in general, they were pictograms and forms masquerading as letters.

I had a sneaking suspicion that these kids couldn't read, much less write. I pulled out a book that I had brought and opened it to the first page. The kids gathered around me, looking up, waiting for me to start reading. I handed the book to Demarcus, who immediately started running around the room, asking me what different things were, and needling Shawn until he got angry and started fighting back. The two girls started pulling things off the craft shelves and asking if they could do art. It was suddenly chaos. It wasn't a sneaking suspicion anymore. They couldn't read. How was I supposed to prepare them to pass a writing test in three hours a week for four months?

I have to admit that I gave up at that moment. I gave up on those kids because I just didn't know what to do. The rest of the four months I spent bringing in books and trying to teach them to read. Maybe, just maybe they would get far enough to . . . what? I didn't know. They weren't going to pass the writing test. There wasn't time, and I didn't know how to teach them. I was so far from their experience. I didn't know what it was like to have a mother in jail or one who cries all the time. I didn't know what it was like to sit in a classroom of kids who can read when you can't. I didn't know what it was like to be ignored as these kids had been.

I gave up on teaching. I decided that I wasn't cut out for it. I dropped out of the teacher education program and decided that the thing for me to do was to take my senior year of college in Mexico. I was going to be a student, nothing more. I didn't really know it at the time, but I was ashamed. I blamed my failure in teaching on the program's not having prepared me for the job presented to me, but it wasn't the program's fault. I blamed myself for not thinking of something immediately that would engage these kids, but I couldn't expect myself to be prepared for that.

In Mexico, I studied the first semester and took the second semester off from school to do some work in a village in the southern part of the country. I could talk for hours about the things I learned from the women in that village, but what stays with me is Angela.

Angela was small for her age and had a terrible case of scabies. The parasite had moved into her face and was making her miserable. Her mother tried to treat it with medicine she got from one of the nurse volunteers who came to the village on the weekends, but she didn't understand how to use it. Rather than putting the cream on once, waiting five days, and putting it on again, she put the cream on her daughter's face every day for an entire week. The chemicals burned the child's face and left her with gaping sores that wouldn't heal.

Angela's mother sent her to live with me and the director of the program in which I was working. I wound up taking care of her most of the time. At first it was kind of charming. We'd walk around the city together, and I got to practice my Spanish and just play a lot of the time. Then she started complaining a lot and stealing money from me, and people would stop me every five minutes to ask what was wrong with her and she would cry. Every night I treated her face with chamomile tea because everything else was too strong for her face to handle. She would lie down on the bed and close her eyes while I washed the burns with cold tea and gauze. I know it hurt her. But I also knew that nothing else would heal her.

One day, as I was washing her face, I was just overcome by a sense of gratitude that I had been put in a place where I had the opportunity to wash this little girl's face. I didn't understand where it came from. I felt so completely fulfilled doing that. I just forgot myself. I forgot myself for a minute, and God slipped in. I had never in my life felt so honest about anything I had done. I knew then that I wanted for my life to be one in which I was real, where I could just forget myself, where I could feel so completely connected with God through touching the burns on a little girl's face.

In that moment, I became a teacher. What had been missing in me when I was working with those fourth graders was a sense that this world is bigger than me. I was selfish, and I didn't know that I was. I thought I was going into teaching to help the world, but really, I was going into teaching to help myself. I thought that if I could inspire children to want to learn, I would be able to inspire myself as well. It didn't work that way.

How could I possibly have imagined that the quote my mom included in my graduation advertisement would come back to me in this way? "We can never do great things, only small things with great love." My mom and Mother Teresa were right. Only when we have cared so deeply that we forget ourselves can we understand how incredibly insignificant we are and at the same time how beautifully essential.

I am working now as the program director for the Self Knowledge Symposium, an organization that seeks to help young people find answers to questions like "Who am I?" Although I do not teach in a classroom, I hope that my work with young people inspires them to be open to finding answers in unlikely places, to accepting the possibility that there is more to this world than meets the eye, and that in order to learn who we truly are, we have to forget ourselves, doing not great things but small things with great love.

*Courage is contagious: When brave men take a stand,
the spines of others are stiffened.*
—BILLY GRAHAM

THE FRONT OF THE BUS

ROSA PARKS

When I got off from work that evening of December 1, I went to Court Square as usual to catch the Cleveland Avenue bus home. I didn't look to see who was driving when I got on, and by the time I recognized him, I had already paid my fare. It was the same driver who had put me off the bus back in 1943, twelve years earlier. He was still tall and heavy, with red, rough-looking skin. And he was still mean-looking. I didn't know if he had been on that route before—they switched the drivers around sometimes. I do know that most of the time if I saw him on a bus, I wouldn't get on it.

I saw a vacant seat in the middle section of the bus and took it. I didn't even question why there was a vacant seat even though there were quite a few people standing in the back. If I had thought about it at all, I would probably have figured maybe someone saw me get on and did not take the seat but left it vacant for me. There was a man sitting next to the window and two women across the aisle.

The next stop was the Empire Theater, and some whites got on. They filled up the white seats, and one man was left standing. The driver looked back and noticed the man standing. Then he looked back at us. He said, "Let me have those front seats," because they were the front seats of the black section. Didn't anybody move. We just sat right where we were, the four of us. Then he spoke a second time: "Y'all better make it light on yourselves and let me have those seats."

The man in the window seat next to me stood up, and I moved to let him pass by me, and then I looked across the aisle and saw that the two women were also standing. I moved over to the window seat. I could not see how standing up was going to "make it light" for me. The more we gave in and complied, the worse they treated us.

People always say that I didn't give up my seat because I was tired, but that isn't true. . . . No, the only tired I was, was tired of giving in.

The driver of the bus saw me still sitting there, and he asked was I going to stand up. I said, "No." He said, "Well, I'm going to have you arrested." Then I said, "You may do that." These were the only words we said to each other. I didn't even know his name, which was James Blake, until we were in court together. He got out of the bus and stayed outside for a few minutes, waiting for the police.

As I sat there, I tried not to think about what might happen. I knew that anything was possible. I could be manhandled or beaten. I could be arrested. People have asked me if it occurred to me then that I could be the test case the NAACP had been looking for. I did not think about that at all. In fact if I had let myself think too deeply about what might happen to me, I might have gotten off the bus. But I chose to remain.

Meanwhile there were people getting off the bus and asking for transfers, so that began to loosen up the crowd, especially in the back of the bus. Not everyone got off, but everybody was very quiet. What conversation there was, was in low tones; no one was talking out loud. It would have been quite interesting to have seen the whole bus empty out. Or if the other three had stayed where they were, because if they'd had to arrest four of us instead of one, then that would have given me a little support. . . .

Eventually two policemen came. They got on the bus, and one of them asked me why I didn't stand up. I asked him, "Why do you all push us around?" He said to me, and I quote him exactly, "I don't know, but the law is the law and you're under arrest."

Keep your fears to yourself, but share your courage with others.
—ROBERT LOUIS STEVENSON

KIDNAP ON A HIGHWAY

JERRY WESTER

A glanced down at my fuel gauge as I drove into the Wal-Mart parking lot. Right on empty. I'd have to stop for gas before picking up my daughter, Erin. I'd promised to take her shopping at the mall.

I didn't feel much like going to the mall that chilly, gray Tuesday afternoon in March. But as a single father unemployed after recent back surgery, I found my life revolving around fourteen-year-old Erin. I adored her. She was a bright spot in my life that otherwise was about as empty as my gas tank.

Within the last year I'd lost almost everything: my physical strength, my job, and finally my marriage of seventeen years. One day my wife just moved out, leaving Erin and me to fend for ourselves. Other than being Erin's dad, I sometimes wondered about my purpose in life.

As I pushed my way through the store's double doors, I glanced at my watch: 4:15. Plenty of time to finish my errand before picking up Erin.

Suddenly an elderly man jostled by me and began talking excitedly. "A woman and her two children were just kidnapped at knifepoint by a man in the parking lot!"

An instinctive anger boiled up inside me. "Where are they now?" I asked.

"There—in that car!" he answered, pointing a shaky finger at a dark blue station wagon heading toward an exit at the far end of the parking lot.

"Does anyone have a cellular phone?" someone asked.

"I do," I answered. Now I kept it in the car in order to be in touch with Erin when she was home alone. Quickly I went outside.

"They turned west onto County Line Road," someone yelled.

I hurried across the lot and jumped into my car. The dark blue wagon disappeared over a hill in the distance as I halted at the exit. Rush-hour traffic was bad. I couldn't see a break in the steady stream of cars. Finally I gunned my way into the line.

Once on the two-lane highway, I began passing cars right and left. Other drivers honked and gestured angrily at me, but I kept going. I had to catch up with that station wagon.

Driving like a maniac, I floored it to 60 on open stretches, then screeched back to 30 to avoid collisions. The road ahead looked like a roller coaster of hills. But still no dark blue car.

Please, God, let me catch them.

It seemed sort of funny to be praying right now. I used to pray regularly, but I'd nearly given up talking to God since my troubles started piling up. The deeper I'd fallen into a downward spiral of difficulties, the farther away from God I felt. Yet now, frantic to help an endangered family, I turned to him automatically.

Up ahead, I saw a red light, so I slowed down, pulled around the stopped cars, looked both ways, and zoomed through the intersection, barely missing an oncoming car. I careered through traffic until I reached the top of another big hill. There it was, a blue wagon, stopped several cars ahead at a red light!

The light changed and the wagon turned left onto C-470, a major four-lane beltway around the west side of Denver. My tires screamed as I lurched through that corner and passed several more cars. The blue wagon melted into the heavy traffic headed toward the mountains.

That's when the doubts started nagging me: *What if this whole chase is a mistake?*

What if that man at Wal-Mart misinterpreted what he saw? This pattern of doubting had become a habit with me lately, usually causing me to withdraw rather than step forward and do something.

Yet I knew I had to catch this car and help these people. With one more burst of speed, I pulled in behind the blue station wagon. I could see a woman driving . . . two children . . . a man in the back seat wearing a dark jacket and stocking cap. He kept sliding around and had something in his hand. A knife? I didn't want him to know I was following them, but I wanted to let the woman know, so when he was looking straight ahead, I quickly flashed my headlights. Did she see? Would she understand my message?

I pulled down my sun visor to hide my face and reached for the phone. Then, thinking of Erin, I glanced at my watch. A little after 4:30. She wouldn't be worried about me yet.

I dialed 911. A dispatcher answered immediately. "Has anyone reported an abduction from the Wal-Mart parking lot in south Denver?" I asked, trying to remain calm.

She paused a moment. "Yes."

"I think I'm following the car," I replied.

"What's the license number?"

I read it to her.

"That's it," she said. "What's your location?"

"We're on C-470, about a mile past University."

"Help is on the way. Can you stay with the car?"

Her question reminded me I was running on empty. "I'm almost out of gas," I told the dispatcher.

"Try to stay with them."

Oh, God, help me, I prayed. *Don't let me run out of gas!*

We'd gone about eight miles and were now in a rural area; traffic had thinned to only a few cars here and there. The sun was disappearing behind the mountains, casting eerie shadows on surrounding hillsides. I strained for signs of patrol cars.

Suddenly the blue station wagon signaled a turn.

"She's getting off at the Ken Caryl Ranch Road turnoff," I barked into the phone.

I followed her down the exit ramp and stopped behind her at a red light. The man looked back. He saw me on the telephone and realized I was following them. He began waving his arms wildly, grabbed the little boy and held something up to the child's throat. I could see terror on the woman's face. The children were crying. This kidnapping was for real.

The blue station wagon suddenly shot through the light and started up the next ramp, headed for C-470 again. Then it pulled over and abruptly stopped, probably a trick to see if I would drive past. I didn't. The woman started and stopped the wagon two more times. I stayed tight on her rear bumper. The kidnapper made some hand motion, and she zoomed back onto the highway. I followed close behind.

"We're back on C-470," I reported.

At that moment, my phone reception crackled and faded. *Oh, no . . . I'm running out of gas and losing phone contact. What now?*

Please, God, help me, I pleaded.

Just then flashing lights glinted in my rearview mirror. I stayed close to the station wagon, hoping the kidnapper couldn't see the lights. Soon the patrol car pulled alongside me. I pointed to the station wagon and dropped back as the officer zipped in between us and with one quick maneuver deftly forced the fleeing car off the highway. The station wagon stopped, and the kidnapper threw down his knife and surrendered.

I looked at my watch: 4:41. It was over. I hurried to the woman; she was sobbing and shaking. "You're okay now," I told her.

In moments the highway came alive with flashing lights. A news helicopter hovered overhead, and television crews arrived for live coverage on the evening news.

Dazed, I made my way back to my car and was able to call Erin. "I'm sorry I'm late, honey," I said, "but turn on the news and you'll see why."

And then the interviews started. The story came together in pieces. The kidnapper had just been released from an Oklahoma state prison and was looking for transportation to Las Vegas. The officers said they never would have found the car in rush-hour traffic if I hadn't followed with my phone. The lady, still shaking, thanked me for saving their lives. Someone called me the cellular phone hero.

When I finally left, a patrolman followed me to the nearest gas station, where my eighteen-gallon tank took more than eighteen gallons of gas.

I was still feeling a bit bewildered when I arrived home. Erin was waiting at the door. "Dad, you were great!" she said, and gave me a hug.

Several days later, the excitement died down and I faced the same old routines and challenges. I hadn't even got what I needed at Wal-Mart. So I drove back to the store, pulled into the parking lot, and sat quietly in my car for a few minutes.

I thanked God that he had allowed me to be in the right place at the right time, not only to help those people, but to show me that no matter how worthless I feel, he still has a purpose for me in life: to be there for others. When I did something to help another, I discovered that God was there for me too . . . even when I was running on empty.

I am only one, but still I am one. I cannot do everything, but still I can do something. . . .
—EDWARD EVERETT HALE

STANDS ARE GOOD, STEPS ARE BETTER
DAVE THOMAS

You don't have to be standing on the front lines of a battlefield pulling the pin out of a grenade with your teeth to be courageous. Sometimes courage is just taking a stand and then backing it up with quiet actions. As a dues-paying member of the Screen Actor's Guild, let me give you some views on what I think being responsible and courageous in the entertainment industry means today.

"Hooray for Hollywood!" some say. Well, not always. Hollywood used to be great at spelling out our dreams or giving us a lift with its jokes and its gags. It's too bad that there's such little good-natured humor left on television or in films. The movies I like are almost all funny ones. I'm a big Bob Hope fan. Who could forget Bob Hope and Jimmy Cagney in their vaudeville dance duet in *The Seven Little Foys?* Or, Bob Hope, Bing Crosby, and Dorothy Lamour in *The Road to Rio?* As for today's actors, I liked Michael Keaton heaps in *Mr. Mom*, but not in *Batman*. Why did they have to do Batman in the bedroom, anyway? Here was a good, old-fashioned role model—the kind that kids still need today—turned into a high-flying playboy. Humor is important, but I don't find that much of what is happening in the entertainment world today is much of a laughing matter.

Wendy's commercials are on television a lot, and that means I am on television a lot. Okay by me, provided I'm hanging out in the right place. That's harder than you may think. "What do you mean by that?" people will ask me. "You guys at Wendy's pay for the ad, don't you? Don't you control where the ad gets put?" The truth is, television schedules change. A football game goes into sudden death overtime or the network runs a news special, and a local station may pull its planned program and shove something else in instead. Sometimes the VCR at the station will break down or the engineer on duty may forget to punch the right button. Then they give an advertiser a "make-good" to make up for the ad that never aired, then watch out!—because make-goods can be bad news. You may have thought you were buying time in *The Adventures of Goldilocks* only to have your ad end up in the middle of *Chainsaw Massacre in Blood Valley*.

In the fall of 1993 some people wrote Wendy's letters about our advertising on national television programs. Unlike many companies, we wrote everybody back and called many of the people who had written in. They were shocked that we took the time, and some were impressed with, or at least understanding of, what we had to say.

Some of the movies we sponsored that the write-in campaign attacked were the slick, raw, and salty films that seem to be what Hollywood churns out and which also win so many Academy Awards year after year. Others, critics say, are works of art—like *The Color Purple*—and deciding whether to sponsor them is a real judgment call. We now have a list of shows on which we won't advertise, including plenty of talk shows and TV tabloids. We even have to watch out which cartoons we buy. A Wendy's ad can show up in *Tom & Jerry*, but I can guarantee you it won't be rubbing shoulders with *Beavis and Butthead*.

We do have controls set up. They work better nationally than they do locally, just because there are so many stations broadcasting across the country these days;

but we're getting better locally too. Still, controls are really not the answer. You're not going to get some pitch from me now on First Amendment rights—although I believe in them. The problem is that not enough entertainment companies out there are funding the making of family entertainment programs. If we all feel this way, the answer is to do something positive.

Why are we concerned? Because the same shows that deliver strong ratings for excessive violence, sex, and profanity for adults deliver an identical audience of teenagers and children.

In a recent Gallup Poll, Americans said there is too much violence on TV, that it is related to the country's crime rate, and the network warning labels do not go far enough in alerting parents to objectionable programming content. Parents are saying they want TV more closely regulated.

Many viewers are also stating they will not buy products advertised in offending shows. In a separate survey, almost two-thirds of adults found television sex and violence offensive. Importantly, nearly half of this group stated they would no longer consider purchasing products advertised in these programs. Therefore, it appears that advertising in a TV show with offensive program content may harm a consumer's perception of a company's image or reputation.

In November 1993, Charlie Rath and I went to New York to the headquarters of ABC/Capitol Cities on Central Park West. We have had a bunch of talks with heads of the networks in recent months, and the topic is always the same: Wendy's wants to encourage the development of more family-oriented and wholesome programming at advertising rates that will attract advertisers. We said we are afraid that Wendy's is going to be shut out of buying advertising time during prime-time network shows because the sex, violence, and foul language on so many prime-time programs doesn't match up with our image as a family restaurant.

We put a number of ideas on the table. We said that it's counterproductive for the networks and big advertisers to be on opposite sides of this debate: People want clean, sensible programming for their families. Families buy the lion's share of the products, and the big companies who make and sell those products want to present them on network television. The networks, we said, should consider carving out dedicated time slots each evening—maybe the first hour or so of prime time—to be used only for family programming, and see if that kind of plan would get backing from major sponsors. My bet is that sponsors of all sorts would rush for that time slot. We also said that we would write a position paper on what we advertisers should do if we are to make advances on the programming content issue.

Our paper—we call it "the white paper"—states that headway in improving television programming will be made only if advertisers take the initiative. In turn, that will only happen when advertisers appreciate that wholesome programming is effective in reaching key audiences. When this truth sinks in, advertisers are sure to sound off against objectionable programs and encourage the success and increasing number of good family programs.

I really expect us to make some progress this way. There's a big lesson here, and it's not about advertising or even about values. It's about standing up for what you believe in. Instead of spending time and energy hollering about what's wrong, figure out what should be right instead, give people the incentive to do the right thing, and start small enough so that you can give the program strong legs and a real base of support. That's what practical courage is all about.

Facing Life's Challenges

*The great virtue in life is real courage
that knows how to face facts and live beyond them.*
—D. H. LAWRENCE

MODEL PATIENT

KAREN DUFFY

When you confront a catastrophic illness, you realize that you have a limited amount of time and a finite amount of energy left to you. Even if you're cured of what ails you, everybody dies of something sooner or later. It's up to you to devote your resources to living an honorable and valuable life. As Marcus Aurelius said, "Make yourself good while life and power are still yours."

Life is made of time, and you can look back on each day as being lost or spent. I've lost too much time to illness to give up any more, and now I'm spending my days to the fullest extent. Disease ignited a passion in me. . . . Now, I'm not so eager to squander my time. . . .

Disease reaffirmed my commitment to service, to my work at the nursing home, because there are people who need love and friendship and companionship more than I need to lie in bed and moan about my suffering. John's gotten involved in some of my do-gooder projects too. Together, we help raise money for the Village Center for Care, which funds the Village Nursing Home as well as a home for people with AIDS who've sold their life insurance early, figuring they'd need the money long before they died. Now, with the new triple therapies, they need a place where they can start learning how to live again instead of waiting for death. Discovering life when you thought only death awaited is something I know a lot about.

I hate to sound corny, but I'm still finding miracles every day. John and I recently became godparents to the son of a close friend. She'd gone through five years of treatment for ovarian cancer, and was finally able to have the child she'd always wanted. Her experience helped rekindle my maternal instincts too.

. . . Experiences like that used to be bittersweet for me, because when I got sick, I thought for a long time that I might not be able to have children. Getting pregnant while on methotrexate would have been impossible. And I was afraid to leave my husband with the burden of children if, you know, I do die. (Plus, there's a tradition in John's family to name the first boy in every other generation Lambros Lambros, and, needless to say, I felt that was a good enough reason in itself to remain childless.) Now I think having a child would be wonderful because it would have a part of John and a part of me, a legacy we'd create together. And after all, if I didn't have sarcoidosis, I could have a child and then get hit by a bus.

If you're in one of those pools where you lay money on which celebrities die in a given year, I hope you don't have me. The bus accident option has recently become a lot more probable (compared to death by sarcoidosis, anyway—I'm not purposely running into traffic or anything). The steroids and methotrexate did their job. My spinal cord lesion is gone.

I recently realized I had a little pink zit on my cheek that hadn't gone away for months. "Do I have sarcoidosis on my skin now too?" I asked Dr. Petito. "Let's just think of it as a little reminder of what happened to you," he said. My central nervous system could develop sarcoid cells again—it's been known to happen. But now I'm under careful medical supervision, and I'll be able to treat it right away, when it's still small. The other day, Dr. Petito hugged me and said, "I think you're going to beat this, I really do. I think you're going to get better."

At a time like this, I try extra hard to laugh at illness, because the humor in these situations is only where you find it. Life won't bring you comfort free of charge. There's no extra credit for being sick, not from fate, the world at large, or your fellow humans.

I have a kind of dual citizenship in the country of the sick and the country of the well. Most days, you wouldn't think I was sick to look at me, yet I have serious medical problems that haven't stopped hurting me. I take my medicine and go to the doctor, but I also go out shopping and model and act. I sometimes feel like I'm an ambassador between the two realms—explaining to healthy people what it's like to be sick, and to sick people how I try to live my life as "healthy" as I can. Most times I can shift back and forthy pretty easily.

. . . Sometimes people tell me I'm brave. "Bravery" is possibly the most overused word in the language, next to "genius." Bravery is putting your life on the line, risking your safety for others. Cops are brave. Soldiers are brave. Baby Jessica wasn't brave just because she'd fallen down a well, and I'm not brave just because I'm sick. Being randomly struck down with a stinking illness, and being forced to deal with it as best I can, isn't brave—it's unlucky. I just paddle as hard as I can with the oars I have.

. . . Mostly, my life now is better than it's ever been. Confronting sarcoidosis forced me to look inside myself and discover who I really am, what my strengths are, and where I want to be. When you come right down to it, there have been a lot of advantages to having a rare and debilitating disease. Unless and until things change for the worst, I'll keep on spittin' in death's eye.

Courage is not the lack of fear. It is acting in spite of it.
—MARK TWAIN

SAVE THE CHILDREN!

E. GENE CRONK

Five-thirty, Tuesday morning, January 17, 1989. I'm jarred awake, soaked in sweat. First dreaming, then awake, I relive my father's death when I was six years old . . . my brother's fatal heart attack . . . the slow death of my mother from cancer.

7:15. Calling our church's intercessory prayer team leader, I blurt out, "I don't know what's wrong. Please pray with me!" She does, intensely, for about fifteen minutes. The suffocating sense of death lets go and I feel better.

8:30. It's a clear, sunny January morning as I drive the five miles to Cleveland Elementary School. I've been a teacher for eighteen years and this is my seventh year teaching all subjects to third-graders. At the first bell, I greet each student, delighted to see their glowing faces. I watch them work their multiplication problems. Math and language periods pass, punctuated by recess.

11:25. Second recess. One other teacher and I have yard duty. My energetic students leap, giggle, and skip onto the playground.

11:30. I walk to the middle of the 200-by-300-foot playground, noticing my yard-duty partner down by the west-end tetherballs, her attention absorbed with a knot of first and second graders. Eight or ten of my students encircle me, grabbing my hands and turning me slowly. I laugh, thinking I must look like a child-powered carousel.

Having just completed a 360-degree yard scan, I'm looking directly southwest at the front corner of an isolated pod of sixth-grade classrooms, when an angry stac-cato *pop-pop-pop* smacks the air fifteen or twenty times. Miranda and Gabriella ask, "Firecrackers?" as my stare is riveted to the ground near the northwest corner of the classroom pod. The ground is erupting with bits of dirt and rock.

In seconds the loud pops start northward across the child-crowded west end of the playground, flashing and biting out chunks of blacktop. Gunfire! The gunman is behind the corner of the building.

Then something I can only describe as a blanket of God's love for the children settles over me, along with the thought that if I get the kids moving eastward right away, we're going to get out of that yard alive! *I've got to save the children!* "Move! Now! Let's go!" I bellow, herding a growing mass of them eighty yards toward the blacktop corridor funneling into the multipurpose room. The *pop-pop-pop* continues behind us.

Suddenly there's a *whooomp!* South of us, a fifty-foot column of smoke and fire rolls skyward as a station wagon bursts into flames. I keep the children moving, about two hundred of them. We're under fire as we all scramble to the multipurpose room.

11:40. I seat the children at tables, trying to calm them and see if everybody's okay. Lunch-duty personnel try to soothe the kindergartners, who were already there. I find Eric on the floor next to the tables moaning, "I'm bleeding. . . . Oh, I'm hurt. . . . He shot me!" Scanning his back and sides, I see no wounds. He gropes toward his right hip. I find an entry wound but no exit wound. "Is it still in me? Am I gonna die?" he asks.

I tell him I think the bullet is still in him, but that he's going to be fine. Our milk-man volunteers, "I'll carry him out for help!" I agree, and he scoops Eric up in his arms.

11:45. Outside, the firing has stopped. "Dear God, let it be over!" I breathe. Six of my boys are missing. I ask if anyone saw them. Some say they saw Karl start to come with us and then run back to check on another student. After that, nobody remem-bers seeing him. I pray for him. The children watch me as if drinking in assurance that everything is going to be okay. We hear helicopters outside. A policeman enters, asks if there are any more wounded children, then leaves. Another policeman enters and directs us to take the children to begin the process of reuniting them with parents.

12:20 P.M. I take the third graders to my classroom. I busy them with writing and drawing paper, while I read to them. I quote the Twenty-third Psalm to them for comfort and pray with them.

Five of my six missing students return to our room, unhurt—they crawled, combat-style, to safety, they tell me. I hug them . . . *but where's Karl?* "He's been shot!" they say. Where? "In the finger!" they all reply, and I heave a big sigh of relief. *Thank you, God. . . . all in my class are alive!*

1:00. We take the children back to the multipurpose room to be reunited with parents. In the room, filled with some 365 students, I seat my class at a large table. It is announced that police will let in ten parents at a time to find their children, to prevent mass panic. We keep lists of who picks up children so we can account for everybody.

1:45. Near me, a Cambodian mother in stone-washed jeans cries out in anguish for her daughter, Sokhim. School aides try to help her locate her daughter. It is almost as though she knows it before the news is confirmed: Her daughter is one of the children killed.

2:00. A small Cambodian girl is crying at the table next to us. I put my hand on her shoulder and ask what's the matter. "Where's my mom and dad?" she asks, sobbing. Telling her that when they come, I'll make sure they find her, I give her a hug. She stops crying. More families arrive to pick up their children. A mixture of joy and tears floods the room. The little girl at the next table still waits, and I wave to her.

2:30. Most of my class have been reunited with parents. Other classes are down to just a few. The Cambodian girl's parents come to pick her up, and I'm overjoyed.

2:45. With only a dozen or so children left, staff members talk among themselves. Teachers from west-wing classrooms remind me of combat veterans, staring absently at times, shaken, perhaps seeing repeating images of the dead and the most seriously wounded, whom they have handled.

3:00. A staff member arrives with an official list: five children killed, twenty-nine children and one teacher wounded. It's been decided we'll resume teaching the next school day, to minimize fears that might develop during an emergency break. Consequently, our custodians must work all night, cleaning up the blacktop and covering the most noticeable bullet holes in classroom walls. Theirs is a lonely job.

I walk back to my classroom as if in a dream. The grounds look strangely quiet, except for an occasional policeman and long strips of yellow tape cordoning off areas.

After straightening my room, I walk to my truck, then drive to meet my wife as flashbacks play in my mind. "God, how I wish I could bring back those five irreplaceable little ones!" Yet I also know that most of the six-, seven-, and eight-year-olds are alive, safe and uninjured. Flooding up from inside comes the prayer, "Thank you, God, and that great big guardian angel that was with us in the yard today!" With so many shots sprayed across the yard full of four hundred children, we have 395 of God's beautiful children alive!

On Wednesday the *Stockton Record* provides a grim report of our ordeal. A twenty-six-year-old drifter with an extensive criminal record had armed himself with an AK–47 assault rifle, donned a flak jacket, and driven to our school. He booby-trapped his station wagon (the explosion I had seen). After firing 105 rounds at the playground, he finally took his own life.

Today I still teach third grade at Cleveland Elementary. I have no idea why evil such as we experienced happens, but I do know one thing: The trauma with which I awoke that day, followed by my call for intercessory prayer, kept me attuned to God all morning. And in the midst of the crisis, God was with me.

*Things turn out best for people
who make the best of the way things turn out.*
—AUTHOR UNKNOWN

ONLY CRABS GO BACKWARDS

FRED EPSTEIN, M.D., AND JOSHUA HORWITZ

On a Sunday morning in late September 2001, I went out for my usual twenty-mile bike ride near my home in Connecticut. That afternoon I was planning to take two of my boys to a Giants football game. I never got there.

I've been told that the front tire of my bicycle hit a depression in the pavement, and I pitched forward over the handlebars. I landed on the pavement headfirst. The impact knocked my brain against the back of my skull, tearing a blood vessel, which caused bleeding over the surface of the brain. I was rushed to the nearest trauma center where a neurosurgeon who happened to be on call was able to remove the blood clot and relieve the pressure on my brain. Although I was wearing a helmet, what truly saved my life was the prompt and expert medical attention I received.

I remained in a coma for twenty-six days.

When I finally regained consciousness, I could only open one eye partway and wiggle my left big toe. I could see my wife, Kathy, and feel her hand holding mine, but I couldn't talk. I couldn't even breathe without the assistance of a ventilator.

I was totally helpless. What I knew was that I couldn't afford to become hopeless.

From years of treating serious head injuries, I was well versed in the rehabilitation drill, and it was no picnic. First I'd have to be weaned off the ventilator. Then

I'd have to learn to swallow. And talk. And walk. I knew I'd have my wife by my side every step of the way, smiling encouragement and squeezing my hand. But I also understood it was going to be a long, uphill climb. And no one besides Kathy was likely to believe I'd make it.

The policeman who came to our house an hour after I was taken to the hospital had told Kathy, "It's critical. Hurry." When I didn't come out of my coma that first week, I'm sure most people—including many of my colleagues who knew the odds—wrote me off for dead. Others thought I would be consigned to what's referred to as a "perpetual vegetative state." The survival rate for an injury like mine is only twenty percent, and only a few emerge from trauma-induced comas after twenty-six days. When they do, their prognosis is grim, especially when they're in their sixties, as I am. Young people tend to do better; their brains are more resilient. I like to think my brain is younger than its biological age because I've always been mentally and physically active. Or maybe I'm just bullheaded.

A week after I revived from my coma, I was moved to a rehabilitation hospital in Manhattan. Gradually—and until I went through rehab for a head injury myself, I never truly grasped the meaning of the word—I began to recover my basic brain functions. I learned to breathe on my own. I learned to swallow. I learned to talk—first in single, barely audible words, then in halting sentences. Right now, I'm learning to walk, one baby step at a time.

. . . I'm back at my own hospital, Beth Israel—not as a doctor but as a patient. After six months at the rehab hospital I was restless to get back to my home base. I still have months of intensive rehab ahead of me. Each day is a grind: speech therapy, followed by occupational therapy, followed by cognitive therapy, followed by physiotherapy for my weak arm and leg. My mind is clear and my spirit is willing, but parts of my body are still not patched into my brain correctly. My right arm and leg are still partially paralyzed, my speech is still slurred, and I have double vision. With time, and more hard work, they'll improve.

Meanwhile, I have to raise the bar another notch for myself every day. I find myself chanting my own "If I get to" mantras to coax myself through the next long session of rehab. If I rehab my right arm well enough, I can play catch with my sons in the backyard. If I get back on my feet, I can sail my boat again on Long Island Sound. If I get my voice back to full strength, I can argue cases with the other doctors at the weekly tumor conferences on the first floor. I'll get back to my old self, I can be a surgeon again. . . .

It's been a year since I revived from my coma. This month, I began going back to work at the Institute for Neurology and Neurosurgery. I'm here only a couple of afternoons a week now, but I'm hoping to build back up to full time and, if my rehab reaches one hundred percent, to get back to the OR. My future role at the INN is still evolving, still a question mark. All I know is that I'm determined to use whatever skills I have to do whatever I can.

My job for the past year has been to rehab my body and mind. In many ways it's been the hardest job of my life. It's given me an even deeper appreciation for the emotional and physical rigors my patients have faced all these years. And it's also given me a poignant insight into the demands it makes on their families.

For most of my adult life I've been in constant motion, shuttling between the OR and patient rounds and tumor boards and medical conferences. This year I've had the rare opportunity to be still, to spend time at home with my family, and to reflect on what I've learned from my practice and from my patients.

I've been on the receiving end of lots of lessons—some tough, some sweet. . . .

But what's been most instructive to me in this season of loss and recovery has been learning what can't be taken away by misfortune.

It's a cliché—and also true—that you really find out who your friends are when you're flat on your back. I've never before been so dependent on the kindness of friends, as well as strangers. Suffice it to say, I've learned who my friends are.

I've spent the last six months almost exclusively at home with my family. My five children, ages fourteen through thirty-two, have taught me hands-on lessons about love this year, each in his or her own way. I have also been blessed with a new granddaughter—and with her birth, I've been reminded that life, like hope, springs eternal.

The cards and letters I've received from my patients this year have been a daily tonic for me. One in particular speaks to my current situation. A young woman quoted her Russian grandfather's proverb that guided her when she was a girl recovering from surgery and trying to regain her direction in life: "Only crabs go backwards."

That pretty much nails it for me. I have to go forward, however uncertain the future—which is, after all, what we all have to do. We fool ourselves into thinking we know what the future holds; in reality, none of us knows what pain or pleasure tomorrow will bring. Choosing to go forward in the face of uncertainty is the willful, distinctly human act of optimism we perform each day. We may know too much about the unpredictable ways of the world to expect a happy ending, but we can't help but hope for one all the same.

*Courage . . . is . . . an affirmative answer
to the shocks of existence.*
—GENERAL WILLIAM T. SHERMAN

PEARL HARBOR

SENATOR DANIEL K. INOUYE

he family was up by 6:30 that morning, as we usually were on Sunday, to dress and have a leisurely breakfast before setting out for nine o'clock services at church. Of course, anyone who has some memory of that shattering day can tell you precisely what he was doing at the moment when he suddenly realized that an era was ending, that the long and comfortable days of peace were gone, and that America and all her people had been abruptly confronted with their most deadly challenge since the founding of the Republic.

As soon as I finished brushing my teeth and pulled on my trousers, I automatically clicked on the little radio that stood on the shelf above my bed. I remember that I was buttoning my shirt and looking out the window—it would be a magnificent day; already the sun had burned off the morning haze and glowed bright in a blue sky—when the hum of the warming set gave way to a frenzied voice. "This is no test," the voice cried out. "Pearl Harbor is being bombed by the Japanese! I repeat: this is not a test or a maneuver! Japanese war planes are attacking Oahu!"

"Papa!" I called, then froze into immobility, my fingers clutching that button. I could feel blood hammering against my temple, and behind it the unspoken protest, like a prayer—*It's not true! It is a test, or a mistake! It can't be true!*—but somewhere in the core of my being I knew that all my world was crumbling as I stood motionless in that little bedroom and listened to the disembodied voice of doom.

Now my father was standing in the doorway listening, caught by that special horror instantly sensed by Americans of Japanese descent as the nightmare began to unfold. There was a kind of agony on his face and my brothers and sister, who had pushed up behind him, stopped where they were and watched him as the announcer shouted on:

". . . not a test. This is the real thing! Pearl Harbor has been hit and now we have a report that Hickam Field and Schofield Barracks have been bombed too. We can see the Japanese planes. . . ."

"Come outside!" my father said to me, and I plunged through the door after him. As my brothers John and Bob started out too, he turned and told them: "Stay with your mother!"

We stood in the warm sunshine on the south side of the house and stared out toward Pearl Harbor. Black puffs of antiaircraft smoke littered the pale sky, trailing away in a soft breeze, and we knew beyond any wild hope that this was no test, for practice rounds of anti-aircraft, which we had seen a hundred times, were fleecy white. And now the dirty gray smoke of a great fire billowed up over Pearl and obscured the mountains and the horizon, and if we listened attentively we could hear the soft *crrrump* of the bombs amid the hysterical chatter of the ack-ack.

And then we saw the planes. They came zooming up out of that sea of gray smoke, flying north toward where we stood and climbing into the bluest part of the sky, and they came in twos and threes, in neat formations, and if it hadn't been for that red ball on their wings, the rising sun of the Japanese Empire, you could easily believe that they were Americans, flying over in precise military salute.

I fell back against the building as they droned near, but my father stood rigid in the center of the sidewalk and stared up into that malignant sky, and out of the depths of his shock and torment came a tortured cry: "You fools!"

We went back into the house and the telephone was ringing. It was the secretary of the Red Cross aid station where I taught. "How soon can you be here, Dan?" he said tensely.

"I'm on my way," I told him. I felt a momentary surge of elation—He wanted me! I could do something—and I grabbed a sweater and started for the door.

"Where are you going?" my mother cried. She was pointing vaguely out the window, toward the sky, and said, "They'll kill you."

"Let him go," my father said firmly. "He must go."

I went to embrace her. "He hasn't had breakfast," she whispered. "At least have some breakfast."

"I can't, Mama. I have to go." I took a couple of pieces of bread from the table and hugged her.

"When will you be back?" she said.

"Soon. As soon as I can."

But it would be five days, a lifetime, before I came back.

The planes were gone as I pumped furiously toward the aid station, more than a mile away. The acrid smell of the smoke had drifted up from Pearl and people, wide-eyed with terror, fumbling for some explanation, something to do, had spilled into the streets. *What would become of them*, I agonized, *these thousands, suddenly rendered so vulnerable and helpless by this monstrous betrayal at the hands of their ancestral land?* In those first chaotic moments, I was absolutely incapable of understanding that I was one of them, that I too had been betrayed, and all of my family.

An old Japanese grabbed the handlebars of my bike as I tried to maneuver around a cluster of people in the street. "Who did it?" he yelled at me. "Was it the Germans? It must have been the Germans!"

I shook my head, unable to speak, and tore free of him. My eyes blurred with tears, tears of pity for that old man, because he could not accept the bitter truth, tears for all these frightened people in teeming, poverty-ridden McCully and Moiliili. They had worked so hard. They had wanted so desperately to be accepted, to be good Americans. And now, in a few cataclysmic minutes, it was all undone, for in the marrow of my bones I knew that there was only deep trouble ahead. And then, pedaling along, it came to me at last that I would face that trouble too, for my eyes were shaped just like those of that poor old man in the street, and my people were only a generation removed from the land that had spawned those bombers, the land that sent them to rain destruction on America, death on Americans. And choking with emotion, I looked up into the sky and called out, "You dirty Japs!"

It was past eight-thirty—the war was little more than half an hour old—when I reported in at the aid station, two classrooms in the Lunalilo Elementary School. I had gained the first six years of my education in this building and before the day was out it would be half-destroyed by our own antiaircraft shells which had failed to explode in the air. Even now confusion was in command, shouting people pushing by each other as they rushed for litters and medical supplies.

Somewhere a radio voice droned on, now and then peaking with shrill excitement, and it was in one such outburst that I learned how the *Arizona* had exploded in the harbor. Many other vessels were severely hit.

And then, at nine A.M., the Japanese came back. The second wave of bombers swooped around from the west and the antiaircraft guns began thundering again. Mostly the planes hammered at military installations—Pearl, Hickam, Wheeler Field—and it was our own ack-ack that did the deadly damage in the civilian sectors. Shells, apparently fired without timed fuses, and finding no target in the sky, exploded on impact with the ground. Many came crashing into a three-by-five-block area of crowded McCully, the first only moments after the Japanese planes reappeared. It hit just three blocks from the aid station and the explosion rattled the windows. I grabbed a litter and rounded up a couple of fellows I knew.

"Where're we going?" one yelled at me.

"Where the trouble is! Follow me!"

In a small house on the corner of Hauoli and Algaroba Streets we found our first casualties. The shell had sliced through the house. It had blown the front out and the tokens of a lifetime—dishes, clothing, a child's bed—were strewn pathetically into the street.

I was propelled by sheerest instinct. Some small corner of my mind worried about how I'd react to what lay in that carnage—there would be no textbook cuts and bruises, and the blood would be real blood—and then I plunged in, stumbling over the debris, kicking up clouds of dust and calling, frantically calling, to anyone who might be alive in there. There was no answer. The survivors had already fled and the one who remained would never speak again. I found her half-buried in the rubble, one of America's first civilian dead of the Second World War. One woman, all but decapitated by a piece of shrapnel, died within moments. Another, who had fallen dead at the congested corner of King and McCully, still clutched the stumps where her legs had been. And all at once it was as though I had stepped out of my skin; I moved like an automaton, hardly conscious of what I was doing and totally oblivious of myself. I felt nothing. I did what I had been taught to do and it was only later, when those first awful hours had become part of our history, that I sickened and shuddered as the ghastly images of war flashed again and again in my mind's eye, as they do to this day.

By the time we had removed the dead to a temporary morgue set up in Lunalilo School, more shells had fallen. It was now, by one of those bitter ironies, that our aid station was hit by our own shells, and we lost precious minutes evacuating what was left of our supplies. Nearby, a building caught fire; and as the survivors came stumbling out, we patched their wounds as best we could and commandeered whatever transportation that passed to get them to the hospital. For those still trapped inside there was nothing in the world anyone could do. The flames drove us back to the far side of the street, and by the time the firemen brought them under control, there was nothing left alive in that burned-out hulk. Then, carrying corrugated boxes, it became our melancholy duty to pick our way through the smoldering beams and hot ashes and collect the charred, barely recognizable remains of those who had perished. We tried to get one body in each box, but limbs came away as we touched them and it was hard to tell an arm from a leg, and so we couldn't always be sure of who, or what, was in any given box.

There are moments I can never forget. An empty-eyed old lady wandered screaming through the wreckage of a house on King street. A boy of twelve or so, perhaps her grandson, tried to lead her from danger, for she could scarcely keep her footing in the ruins. But the old woman would not be budged. "Where is my home?" she would cry out hysterically in Japanese, or "Where are my things?"

I climbed up to where she tottered on a mountain of wreckage and took hold of her shoulders. "Go with the boy," I said to her.

But it was as though I wasn't there. She looked right through me and wailed, "What have they done to my home?" And without thinking about it, for if I had thought about it I could never have done it, I slapped her twice across the face, sharply. Later, I would be awed by my audacity—my whole life had been a lesson in reverence for my elders—but at that instant I remembered only what I had been taught to do in cases of uncontrollable hysteria. And it worked.

"Go with the boy," I said again, and the light of reason returned to her eyes, and she went.

... We worked on into the night, and were working still when the new day broke. There was so much to be done—broken bodies to be mended, temporary shelter to be found for bombed-out families, precautions against disease, food for the hungry, and comfort for the bereaved—that even our brief respites for a sandwich or a cup of coffee were tinged with feelings of guilt. We worked on into the following night and through the day after that, snatching some broken moments of sleep wherever we happened to be when we could move no further, and soon there was no dividing line between day and night at all.

Each day the world is born anew for him who takes it rightly.
—JAMES RUSSELL LOWELL

FACING MY NEW LIFE

CHRISTOPHER REEVE

Soon I realized that I'd have to leave Kessler [Rehabilitation Center] at some point. A tentative date was set for sometime between Thanksgiving and mid-December. I thought, *God, I've totally given up on breathing. So what am I going to do, stay on a ventilator for the rest of my life?*

There were other possibilities. One option was phrenic pacing, a drastic and dangerous procedure. Batteries are surgically inserted into your chest to stimulate the diaphragm. After the implantation you have to stay in intensive care for months of constant monitoring. The risks are enormous. Batteries fail. Phrenic nerves can be damaged by the constant electrical impulses. The procedure frees you from a ventilator, but the outcome can be fatal. Other techniques were suggested to me, but none of them worked very well. A mouthpiece could be rigged on my wheelchair. I would have to take a breath through the mouthpiece, then turn to the sip-and-puff on my chair and try to drive it. The idea was to gradually reduce dependence on the ventilator. But the breath control needed to operate the chair would have made this far too complicated and dangerous. I could just see myself driving along, then turning my head for a breath from the mouthpiece and losing control of the chair. So I dismissed that idea as well.

But my diaphragm had been doing nothing since May, and now it was the end of October. From my study of the spinal cord handbook, I was aware that if I allowed it to atrophy, I might never be able to use it. I decided I *had* to make another attempt to breathe on my own.

They brought in Dr. Thomas Finley from Kessler's research department. He wanted to place electrodes all over my chest to see if there was any muscle activity that would give some hope. But Dr. Kirshblum advised against it, because of the danger of puncturing a lung when the electrodes were inserted.

I announced that on the first Monday of November, I was going to try again to breathe on my own. At three-thirty in the afternoon of November 2, Bill Carroll, Dr. Kirshblum, Dr. Finley, and [my therapist] Erica met me in the physical therapy room. And I remember thinking: This is it. I've *got* to do something, I have simply *got* to. I don't know where it's going to come from, but I've *got* to produce some air from someplace.

Dr. Finley said, "We're going to take you off the ventilator. I want you to try to take ten breaths. If you can only do three, then that's the way it is, but I want you to try for ten. And I'm going to measure how much air you move with each breath, and let's just see where you are. Okay?"

And I took ten breaths. I was lying on my back on the mat. My head moved up as I struggled to draw in air—I wasn't able to move my diaphragm at all, just my chest, neck, and shoulder muscles in an intense effort to bring some air into my lungs. I was only able to draw in an average of fifty cc's with each attempt. But at least it was something. I had moved the dial.

We came back the next day, and now I was really motivated. I prepared myself mentally by imagining my chest as a huge bellows that I could open and close at will. I told myself over and over again that I was going home soon and that I couldn't leave without making some real progress. Dr. Finley asked me to take another ten breaths for a comparison with yesterday's numbers. I took the ten breaths, and my average for each one was 450 cc's. They couldn't believe it. I thought to myself: All right. Now we're getting somewhere.

At three-thirty the next day I was in place and ready to begin, but several members of the team were late. I thought, *Come on, we're going to have discipline here, we've all got to get together if we're going to make this happen.* Finally I was really taking charge. When Dr. Finley arrived, once again he asked me to take ten breaths. This time the average was 560 cc's per breath. A cheer broke out in the room.

And the next day we met again. All along Dr. Finley had been telling me when to breathe. He'd say, "Let it out. And breathe. And let it out, and breathe." But now I suggested that I might do better if I just timed my own breaths when I felt the need for more air. So he took off the hose, and I started again. I was gasping, sucking for air, and my eyes were rolling up in my head. It was a maximum effort, psychologically and physically. But I breathed on my own for seven and a half minutes.

When I got up to the west wing near my room, [respiratory therapist] Bill Carroll was beside himself. He said, "I've never seen progress like that. You're going to wean. You're going to get off this thing." For the first time I thought it might be possible.

After that Erica and I worked alone. Every day we would breathe. I went from seven minutes to twelve to fifteen. Just before I left Kessler on the thirteenth of December, I gave it everything I had, and I breathed for thirty minutes. I remember Dr. Kirshblum saying, "I don't know how you're doing this, but then I don't know how you do a lot of what you do." The previous summer, still adjusting to my new circumstances, I had given up. But by November I had the motivation to go forward.

Something else happened to me during those months, which was as therapeutic as any physical progress. When I first came to Kessler, I wanted no part of the disabled population. Gradually I had come to see that not only was I part of it but I might be able to do something important for all of us. I began to think that I could be useful to the scientists who were searching for a cure for paralysis. I had begun to understand something about the special character of celebrity. Although I had made several more "serious" movies, such as *The Remains of the Day*, it was clearly my portrayal of Superman that the public had taken to. I knew this role had a unique resonance and had won a great deal of affection for me, for which I had always been grateful. And it seemed that my injury, if anything, had created a new level of public support.

No one was specifically saying, "You could lead the charge on spinal cord disorders," but hearing from certain people helped me formulate the idea. I was visited by Dr. Wise Young of New York University–Bellevue Medical Center, one of the great pioneers in spinal cord research, and by Arthur Ullian, an activist who had been paralyzed from the waist down in a bicycle accident. Arthur has been lobbying Congress for years, and they were the first to impress upon me the unique role that I could play. At about the same time I was contacted by Henry Steifel, chairman of the American Paralysis Association, asking if I might find a celebrity host for their annual fund-raising dinner that November. I was able to enlist Paul Newman, and with his participation the dinner was a tremendous success.

[My friend and aide] Juice had often told me, "You've been to the grave two times this year, brother. You're not going there again. You are here for a reason." He thought my injury had meaning, had a purpose. I believed, and still do, that my injury was simply an accident. But maybe Juice and I are both right, because I have the opportunity now to make sense of this accident. I believe that it's what you do *after* a disaster that can give it meaning.

I began to face my new life. On Thanksgiving in 1995, I went home to Bedford to spend the day with my family. In the driveway, when I saw our home again, I wept. Dana held me. At the dinner table, when each of us in turn spoke a few words about what we were thankful for. Will said, "Dad."

It is in changing that things find purpose.

—HERACLITUS

GROUNDED

SUE PALMER

I was seven stories above the ground, straddling a steel girder, welding pipes in the blistering August heat, when a shudder of dizziness went through me. I cut off the flame of my welder and raised my visor. For eleven years I'd worked as a steamfitter on high-rise construction jobs, soldering joints and making sure the heating systems of the buildings were solid. There weren't too many of us female pipe fitters, but I loved my job all the same. Usually I liked the high vantage point, but that day I felt a little queasy looking down. By quitting time I was ready to head home and curl up with a good book—and my brood of purring cats.

I hadn't intended to take in nine, but somehow kitties who needed homes seemed to find their way to mine. That night my buddy Izzy-Pooh curled beside me as I read. He's white with a black tail and two distinctive black marks between his ears. I'd rescued Izzy when he was a kitten, from a man who was using him for backyard target practice. When the fuzzy little cat was diagnosed with distemper and was on the verge of death, I tended him round the clock, calling the vet for advice and asking over and over, "Is he going to make it? Is he . . . ?" The kitten recovered. And I'd asked "Is he?" so many times that it seemed right to name him Izzy. Izzy-Pooh.

That night after work, even a good book and Izzy's company couldn't distract me from my blinding headache. Then I noticed a hair on the page—not unusual for a person with cats. When I brushed the page, however, the hair remained. Okay, I thought, rubbing my eyes, I need some rest. But the next morning the line in my vision was still there, and worse.

An ophthalmologist diagnosed the problem as a swelling of the optic nerve in my left eye. Even after surgery, I never saw out of that eye again. For several months I tried to continue as a steamfitter, but my headaches got worse, and with sight in only one eye, I had no depth perception. It was too dangerous for me to continue at my job. I had to get my feet on the ground and keep them there. Heartsick, I took permanent disability leave.

My disability payments, however, weren't enough to live on. When I ran into a friend who was a secretary at the local newspaper, I tried to joke about my predicament. "If you ever quit," I said, "I want your job."

"How did you know?" she asked. "I'm leaving town. My job is up for grabs now."

Trade in my construction boots for sensible shoes? A steamfitter turned secretary? I applied for the job and got it. It worked out well. After a while I had an idea and went to the editor with it.

"You want to write what?" she asked, not looking up from the copy she was scribbling on.

"A cat advice column," I explained.

"You want to give advice to cats?"

"No, no, to their owners."

Finally the editor said okay. I talked to vets and corresponded with readers, enjoying it immensely. People started calling me the cat lady.

All was going well, until the headaches returned, with a searing vengeance. Tests revealed I had a meningioma, a potentially fatal tumor that feeds on and can destroy the meninges, the sheaths covering the nerves in the body. After getting second and third opinions and doing extensive research, I had to face the fact that surgery was the only solution.

The risks were enormous. Even though the surgery could save my life, it might also result in permanent blindness or paralysis. Lying on a gurney in the hospital hallway awaiting my operation, I had never felt so helpless. *What if I wake up unable to think? To move? To see? What if . . . ?* I felt dizzy, just as I had that day high on the girder. In the next moment, though, words came: *Trust in the Lord with all your heart.* Gradually a sense of peace as warm as the sun enveloped me.

When next I opened my eyes, the room swam into view. A nurse stood beside my bed. "Water, please," I requested weakly, then wiggled my fingers and toes. I could still see, think, speak, and move! I had a headache, but I was alive. Before long the doctor appeared. "We removed as much of the tumor as we could," he said gently. "But we weren't able to get all of it." Later he told me there was a possibility it might grow back. "In the meantime," he said, "go home and rest and get strong."

As I recuperated at home, my elation at coming through the operation was overtaken by anxiety. How was I going to pay my medical bills? Would the tumor come back? What could I do to make more money? The frightening questions raced: What if . . . ? How . . . ? Is . . . ?

Izzy. Izzy-Pooh was under the afghan with me, lying next to my leg, purring as I petted him. I scooped him into my arms and began to cry. The eight other cats gathered around and gently rubbed against me. They seemed to say, "You've asked questions long enough. It's time to listen to some answers." I took a deep breath. "Lord," I prayed, "what am I going to do now?"

The answer came clearly: Do what you love.

Izzy looked up and put his ears back as though he were thinking things over right along with me. The two black patches on his head looked for all the world like velvety hearts.

What did I love? I loved cats! A voice spoke to me again: *Take care of my cats.* I laughed. I could do that! After all, I was the cat lady. While people were at work or on vacation, I could go to their homes and check on their kitties. That wasn't all.

Excitedly I grabbed a pen and paper and drew up a list of services: feed and change water, clean litter box, spend quality time playing with kitties—and while I was at it, water plants or bring in the mail. The ideas came so rapidly I could barely keep up. I could help with medication and problem behavior. I could provide information for first-time cat owners, and help introduce new cats into a household. As my own cats curled around me, I thought of what to call my business: The Cats' Asset. That's what I was, all right. I could make a go of it.

I put an ad in the paper. Particularly since my column had made me something of an expert, responses began pouring in. Some owners wanted me to make house calls while they were away, others needed backup in giving shots or supplying extra attention to geriatric cats.

In 1996 I went into business full-time. Now things are, well, purring. I also run a coffee shop at my church, with proceeds going to local animal shelters.

I loved what I did; now I do what I love. Even if my health falters again, I know things will turn out fine, because what grounds me is an assurance far sturdier than the steel I used to weld. I trust in the Lord, who has shown me he can teach even an old cat lover some new tricks.

Trusting *in* God

Without the assistance of the Divine Being . . .
I cannot succeed. With that assistance, I cannot fail.
—ABRAHAM LINCOLN

CAPSIZED!

DEBRA LAUGHLIN

isitors flock to North Carolina beaches every year, and in the spring of 1997, the Camarerros were no exception. German and Oliva, the parents of our fifteen-year-old Spanish exchange student, also named Oliva, had come from Madrid, Spain, for a two-week visit with their daughter, and the beach was high on their list of must-see stops. So one unseasonably warm spring day, I took my two children, John, seven, and Emily, three, and the Camarerros to visit my parents at their beach home in Aydlett, North Carolina, about fifty miles from where we lived.

The eight of us decided to take advantage of the beautiful weather by donning our swimsuits and boarding my father's twenty-foot, Coast Guard–approved deck boat to head across Currituck Sound to the unspoiled beaches of Corolla, a remote barrier island resort, for fun in the sun. After a twenty-minute boat ride there, we explored Corolla's lighthouse, gathered seashells, and took advantage of some great photo opportunities.

After about an hour, we felt hungry. German had promised to make us Spanish paella for lunch, so we boarded the boat and set sail for home. Although the wind had picked up some since we'd arrived, no one was worried; the weather forecast had been fine. Yet the waters of the sound seemed choppier; sprays of water whipped at the boat's hull, bouncing upward and soaking us.

It's going to be a long, wet ride home, I thought. I had no idea how right I was.

As we approached the middle of the sound, dark clouds filled the sky. Winds began topping at forty miles per hour, while waves crested at three to four feet. Since my father's a seasoned boater, at first I wasn't too concerned. But as our boat struggled in the water, a sense of foreboding overtook me. Why was the motor working overtime—with so little progress against the pummeling waves and winds? Unbeknownst to us, the hull of my father's boat had cracked because of a manufacturer's defect, and water was pouring in.

As John and Emily huddled beside me, shivering, Oliva moved to the back to sit with her mother. Before long, waves cascaded over the back of the boat. John and Emily started crying; anxiety appeared on the Camarerros' faces, as well as my mom's. Since Oliva's parents spoke no English and we spoke no Spanish, I flashed them the "okay" sign to keep them calm. Then, fighting my own fear, I pulled my children close to me and breathed a quick prayer: "Lord, please see us through this."

Water started pouring in, overwhelming the boat's bilge pump. As I helped German bail out the water, I remembered a Bible verse I'd recently memorized: "When I am afraid, I will trust in you. In God, whose word I praise, in God I trust; I will not be afraid" (Psalm 56:3–4). I repeated it as I frantically bailed the last of the water out of the tossing boat. Just as I caught my breath, I noticed the boat was listing to the right.

"Dad!" I yelled, "The boat is leaning!"

My father immediately lifted the hatch and saw the equivalent of two thousand gallons of water in the hull. He quickly handed out life jackets and commanded everyone to get into the center of the boat in an attempt to stabilize it.

"Get your jackets on, we're going into the water!" he shouted. I couldn't believe it.

"No, Dad, no!" I shouted back. "You can fix anything!"

"Debbie, it's over," my dad said with quiet reserve. At that, our exchange student, Oliva, became hysterical. John cried, "Mommy, I don't want to die!" Emily just screamed. *This must be a very bad dream*, I told myself.

As the boat leaned to the left, we shifted to the right like little crabs. But the motion of the water in the hull, the waves and the wind, were too much for the crippled vessel. I grabbed Emily's hand as well as an extra life jacket, and we crept to the top of the boat—Titanic-like—to delay the inevitable: being plunged, slow-motion, into the salty, fifty-degree water. When the boat capsized, my dad hit the water first. I lost sight of John. Emily and I were tossed in the cold, dark water; it felt as though I'd landed on a thousand knives. The water consumed me like a large monster. As I fought my way to the surface, separated from Emily, I knew instantly she'd gotten trapped under the boat. I dove under to rescue Emily, but when we emerged, my life-jacket cord caught on some underwater object. I couldn't get to the surface. I panicked. Instead of thinking unsnap and untie, I frantically ripped at my jacket and desperately tried to reach the surface. Finally, miraculously, whatever held me under released its hold—and I was free.

On the surface, there was pandemonium—screaming and crying. A small piece of boat remained floating and my mother, John, Emily, Oliva, and her mom scrambled on top, coughing and choking on the salty water. My dad frantically did a quick head count as he floated in the rough, frigid water with German and me: eight. We were all there. But despite my life jacket, I was floundering. Just six weeks earlier, another boating tragedy on the same body of water had claimed four other lives, two of whom were children. *Here we are, facing the same untimely death*, I thought. *This is how we're going to die.*

No one else was boating that day. No one knew we were boating. We had no flares. We had no radio. No rescue was imminent. I knew I was a strong swimmer—I'd been a lifeguard in high school—so when I asked my mother out of desperation if I should try to swim to shore, she said, "Yes! Go!"

As I headed toward mainland, German insisted he join me. Within minutes we lost sight of the boat. Even though we both had life jackets, waves continually pulled us under. When we'd resurface another wave would pummel us back down. Although German and I tried to stay together, the wind and waves separated us. We called out until we found each other again and resumed the treacherous journey.

At one point, I started to choke on seawater and panic rose in my throat. I knew if I let it out, it would consume me. German swam over to me, grabbed me, and said firmly, "No, no, Debra! *Tranquila, tranquila*!" (the Spanish word for calm).

We'd been into our swim about an hour and a half when I started growing weary and cold. As my legs cramped, I began to think I'd made a mistake by leaving the boat. Shore was still so far away. Because of the panic, I hadn't said goodbye to my children. I hadn't told them I loved them. I'd just swum away.

I also thought of my husband, John, a navy pilot deployed in the Persian Gulf. He'd have to come home and bury his family.

With every stroke I took, I said a prayer. I mentally recited every Bible verse and sang every hymn I could remember. I begged God for mercy; I begged him for strength. I begged him for my children's lives. I prayed, "God, please, please, please see us through this!"

Back on the boat, John and Emily huddled between my mom and Oliva. My father remained in the water, holding onto a rope tied to the boat. It had been three hours since German and I'd left, and they were beginning to despair. My father started to cry, telling my mom he was sorry. He felt it was his fault; he also told her he thought German and I had been gone too long; he was certain we were dead. My dad tied himself to the wreckage, telling my mom not to untie him. He didn't want to float around for days, dead and undiscovered.

But what my father didn't know was that German and I did make it, just as the sun was setting—two and a half hours after we first set out. We hit shore at four-thirty P.M. and flagged down a cyclist, who alerted the neighbors. German and I were carried into a neighbor's home, then treated for hypothermia at the Coast Guard station.

Within minutes, the shore was filled with police, rescue workers, and the Coast Guard, who sent out their rescue helicopter.

Fifteen-year-old Oliva was the first to spot the helicopter. She pointed and cried, "Helicopter! Helicopter!" Everyone on the boat began to cry and wave their arms in the air. First the helicopter circled, then dropped a rescue swimmer in the water with a basket. All six were safely airlifted out of the water and taken to the Elizabeth City Coast Guard Station, where we were reunited.

One hour later, the boat sank. Nine days later, it washed to shore.

Three weeks later, I returned to my parents' beach house. My dad had retrieved the remains of the boat; it was devastating to see the wreckage. I visited the pier where German and I were pulled from the water. Currituck Sound looked calm and beautiful. As I stood on the pier and looked over what could have been our watery grave, I noticed a twelve-foot cross to the right of the pier. It had been erected for Easter Sunday; I hadn't noticed it the day of the accident because I was so distraught. Suddenly I felt overwhelmed by the presence of God and awed by how my prayers for survival had been answered.

We're still reeling from the trauma of the boating accident. My children remain terribly afraid of wind, boats, and dark water. Last year, we had dinner with my husband on the aircraft carrier *Enterprise*, and Emily asked if the boat would tip over.

But this experience has given us a special bond with the Camarreros. We call each other monthly, and Oliva came back to visit this summer. We frequently talk of the incident, and of how grateful we are to be alive.

Recently our pastor talked about being thankful. "Can you thank God for an experience, even if you never know why it happened?" he asked us. At the time of the boating accident, I couldn't fathom why it was happening. As a new Christian, I didn't feel ready to die, or for my children to die. But now I know God was teaching me about his glory and faithfulness.

An extraordinary event? Yes. A supernatural work of God? I believe so. Today I celebrate life—and thank God for giving us each new day!

Walk boldly and wisely . . .
There is a hand above that will help you on.
—PHILIP JAMES BAILEY

THE WARNING

RENIE SZILAK BURGHARDT

hroughout the years of World War II, in our country, Hungary, my grandparents and I managed to survive, although we had many close calls. But when that terrible war finally ended in 1945, there was no jubilation for the people of Hungary, because Soviet troops occupied our land and held our country hostage in the arms of communism. Suddenly, people who spoke out against new oppressions that began to take place were rounded up by the newly formed secret police and never seen again!

My grandparents had raised me. My grandfather, a retired judge, was not afraid to speak out, and one day, in the fall of 1945, two men appeared at our house to take him away. They said he was being taken in for questioning only. Grandfather, pointing out that his hands were dirty from working in the garden, asked the men if he could wash up first. The men agreed. When he didn't come out of the bathroom within a few minutes, the men ran and pushed the door open. The water in the sink was still running, but Grandfather had disappeared! He had managed to jump out the bathroom window and flee on foot. The two men raced out the door and up and down our street, looking for Grandfather, while my grandmother held me close as we tearfully prayed for Grandpa's safety.

Grandfather managed to elude capture and went into hiding, while life became more and more difficult for Grandmother and me. We lived on soup made from a few vegetables that grew in our garden, and we never knew when the secret police would show up at our house again, in hopes of finding Grandpa. Sometimes they came in the middle of the night, breaking down our door. Fear became our constant companion then, and prayer became our sustenance.

For two years my grandfather managed to elude capture, and although eventually he sent word to us that he was safe, most of the time we didn't know his whereabouts. Grandmother and I missed him terribly. The thought that we might never be together again plagued me constantly. But on an autumn day in 1947, when I was almost ten years old, I knew exactly where to find him, and it seemed as though the time had come for us to be reunited.

The day before, new elections had been held in our country, and I waited for the results with hope in my heart. So the morning after the elections, when our radio broadcast announced that the communist party had been defeated, I was overjoyed! Celebrations erupted in the streets too, with none of us realizing that the communist government, backed by the Soviet troops, wasn't about to give up power, elections or no elections.

But after listening to the radio, my almost ten-year-old mind concluded the election results meant that Grandfather could come home and we could be a family again. I immediately wondered if Grandfather, who we recently learned was hiding out on a nearby farm, had heard the news. I decided now was a good time to hike out to the farm and tell him. Then we could come home together and surprise Grandma.

Of course, I didn't tell anyone of my plan. Rather than go to school, I set out on the long walk to Grandfather's hiding place. As I reached the outskirts of our village without drawing any attention to myself, wild anticipation filled my heart. In a short while I would see Grandfather for the first time in over two years, and we would walk home together and live as a family again. My eyes filled with tears of joy with that thought, and I began to walk faster.

Suddenly I was startled when I heard a man's voice calling my name. I stopped dead in my tracks and looked all around me, but saw no one. "Who are you? Where are you? I can't see you," I asked, straining to see if the speaker might be behind some nearby bushes.

"It isn't important where I am," the voice said. "I am here to warn you that you are about to put your grandfather in grave danger, for you are being followed. Turn around and go back to your grandmother immediately, and know that you all will be together, soon."

Of course, very frightened now, I immediately turned and began running back toward the village, my heart pounding so hard I thought it would jump right out of my chest. I ran past a man on a bicycle and recognized him as one of the secret police who had been at our house. The stranger's voice had been right: I was being followed!

When I reached our house, I found Grandma outside, pacing back and forth in the street. "Oh, thank God, you are all right!" she cried when she saw me, gathering me in her arms. "They came to tell me that you were not in school, and I thought someone had taken you away."

"I decided to go and tell Grandfather that the communists lost the election," I wailed. "I thought we could come home together and surprise you!"

"Oh, my!" Grandma said, shaking her head in disbelief. "Oh, my!"

"But someone stopped me," I continued excitedly, tears streaming down my face. "A voice told me I was being followed and that I should run back home. It was the kindest, most loving voice I have ever heard, Grandma. I think it was the voice of God, speaking to me. No one, but no one else, knew of my plan!"

My grandmother nodded silently, ushered me into the house and, while holding me close, reassured me that everything would be better soon.

Two weeks later, a man came to get us in the middle of the night. By the time the sun rose, we had traveled many miles to a place near the Austrian border where a large group of ethnic Germans were about to be deported into Austria. My heart leapt with joy when I saw Grandfather there. He looked into my eyes lovingly and hugged me tightly. We were to be smuggled out of our country as ethnic Germans.

Aware of the danger still around us, we didn't dare breathe a sigh of relief until we crossed the border. In Austria, we ended up in a refugee camp along with hundreds of other destitute refugees, but at least we were finally together again as a family.

Grandfather remained fearful that the long arm of communism could still reach out and snatch him back. It wasn't until 1951, when we were given the chance at new lives in a wonderful new country, the United States of America, that he was finally able to relax and live out his life in grateful peace.

Over the years, I often wondered about the voice I heard on that fall day in 1947. Could the voice have belonged to some kind neighbor who had guessed my destination, and decided to warn me anonymously? Or perhaps it really was the voice of God that prompted me to turn around. But whether the voice was human or heavenly, of this I am certain: it was God's hand that guided us safely back together so we could be a family again.

*I know not by what methods rare, but this
I know: God answers prayer.*
—ELIZA M. HICKOK

THE DECISION

CINDY BARKSDALE

Not all mothers are blissfully happy when their first child is born. For some, the circumstances are difficult and confusing. That was the case the night my girlfriend dropped me off at St. Anthony's Hospital. Alone and afraid, I was taken to a small room and told to put on a gown and lie on the bed. The nurses didn't speak much to me—I was unmarried, young, alone, and pregnant, and such a thing was frowned upon, especially in the South in the early 1970s. Alone I bore the heaviness of the labor of childbirth in a darkened labor room, only occasionally checked by nurses who didn't show much compassion.

Little did I know of the workings of such a place—of what had already been planned for me. The hospital had a social service director, and when an unmarried, teenage girl came in to give birth, they had a deserving family already in mind for the new child. They would help me see how inadequate and unprepared I was for childbirth, much less for parenthood. And of course they were right.

After my delivery, I woke from a deep sleep. In the dark hours before dawn, I looked around the room: old linoleum yellowed on the floor beneath my railed bed, one small light on the wall behind me, a metal chair against the wall. Where was my baby? Was it a girl, a boy? I cried out, and in my drug-induced state, I vaguely remembered my mother bending over me. "It's a girl," she whispered. "She is healthy and beautiful."

When I awoke some hours later I rang for the nurse and asked for my baby. She seemed puzzled, but after much persistence on my part, she brought in a small bundle and laid her in my arms. The baby was so beautiful, so small, so perfect. Thick, dark curly hair topped her round pink face. Her eyes were as dark as raisins, and her skin was as smooth as the finest silk. A baby! A little person! My mind was swirling with thoughts and my heart overflowing with emotions. I had no idea what I was doing, but this I did know: my life would never be the same.

Soon after, a social worker came to visit me. She explained that they had a family, a special and loving family who had been waiting for so long for a child they could love and care for. She talked to me about responsibility, my future, and the opportunities I would lose trying to raise a baby alone. Much of what she said was true. I was so young—only sixteen years old—but I felt deep in my soul that this was the most important decision I would perhaps ever make.

I told her I would pray. I didn't know much about prayer. I had been to church as a young girl with my grandmother. There had certainly been times when I had prayed in the past, "Please get me out of this mess" but I knew this was a different kind of prayer. I needed an answer. I waited for it. I listened, day after day I listened, with the social worker encouraging me to do the responsible thing for this little girl. Each afternoon, friends visited me, quiet about their opinions. Each evening my mother and grandmother visited, also quiet. Everyone was waiting for me. I was waiting for God.

After nine days the pressure was mounting. The hospital wanted my bed. The social services wanted my baby. I wanted my answer. One afternoon my girlfriend tiptoed into my room. She sat on the side of my bed and took my hand in hers.

Eyes brimming with tears, she shared her hidden secret with me. She too had been an unwed, teenage mother. She too had faced this decision. She too had been afraid. In heartbreaking detail she described her feelings and concerns at the time. She knew exactly how I was feeling. She told me that now, at age twenty-one, she knew in her heart that letting go of her baby to a loving and wonderful family had been the right thing to do, and she encouraged me to do the same. She left, and I was alone with my thoughts. I had prayed for God to give me an answer. Was this it? Logically it made sense. It must be right, but what was wrong with my heart? It felt like it was breaking.

That night my mother came again to see me. She had kept her opinions to herself as I had struggled over the past few days, waiting for an answer to my prayers. She knew more, saw more, felt more than she shared with me. It would be many years later when she would confirm the events of that night with me.

I had been waiting for her to come. All afternoon I'd cried. I told my mother of the visit with my friend, of the story she had shared. I told her that after talking to my friend I had decided to let my baby go home with the family that waited for her. I had decided in my mind, but what was I going to do about my heart? The feelings there were quite different. I felt as if I was grieving. I felt something had died inside of me.

At last, my mother began to share her feelings with me. She did not agree with my girlfriend and told me of her own impressions over the past several days. I don't remember much of what she said, for I was listening—listening to the sound of my baby crying in the nursery. I got up and walked down the corridor to the baby nursery at the end of a long hall. It didn't occur to me that it would have been impossible for me to hear a baby crying so far away and in an enclosed room, much less to distinguish the sound of my own crying child. But somehow I just knew she was crying and that I needed to go to her.

I was not aware of my mother following me down the hall to the nursery—I was conscious only of the sound of my daughter's cry.

As I peered through the glass wall that separated me from my crying child, a bright, white light seemed to descend from the ceiling above her and encompassed the crib in which she lay. It was luminous and shone directly on her little body. Then I heard these words, as clearly as if someone were speaking in my ear. "This is your child. She was sent here to you. No one will ever be able to love her as you will." Suddenly, joy swelled within my heart and peace filled my aching soul, and I knew God had truly heard and answered my prayers. The next morning, a long ten days after her birth, I took my precious daughter home with me.

The years that followed were certainly not easy. I worked as a waitress, spent two years in college, and made many mistakes along the way. I know the decision to keep the baby would not be right for many young women; giving up a baby for adoption is a noble act of love. And yet time after time, the voice I heard and the light I saw that night gave me the courage to know I had done the right thing for this particular baby.

I had been given a clear understanding that this child would need my love and devotion in her life. But what soon become even more evident was that I would need her love and support to carry me through some difficult years. That daughter has now graduated from college and is making a wonderful life on her own. I cannot imagine what my life would have been without her.

Keep strong if possible; in any case, keep cool.
—SIR BASIL LIDDELL HART

RESCUE ON THE SUNSET LIMITED

LILLIAN BEECH

t 2:30 A.M. on September 22, 1993, I stood on the fog-shrouded train platform at the Mobile, Alabama, Amtrak station, waiting to board the *Sunset Limited*, a superliner bound for Miami. I'd never been on a double-decker superliner before, so I stepped cautiously in the dimly lit passageway as I followed the conductor. He stowed my suitcase, then led me up a flight of stairs.

In the darkened upper passenger compartment I could barely make out the heads of sleeping passengers. I groped toward two empty seats not far from the stairwell. As I settled in, the train eased out of the station with a lazy sway.

I was on my way to Florida to babysit my daughter's children. At sixty-seven I was as busy as ever. I'd raised four children, continued to help run the family concrete business, and could still coax a dose of cough syrup down any one of my ten grandchildren.

I said a prayer, as I always do when starting a trip, and pulled a blanket around me. I pray about everything. I knew that when I prayed, God heard my voice. But that past Sunday in church as I listened to the pastor's sermon, I wondered if I listened closely enough for God's voice. After all, listening is a form of prayer too. Now, as the lights outside passed by faster and faster, I listened for God's voice—and dropped off to sleep.

Bam! I was jarred awake by a terrible explosion and the shriek of twisting metal.

Then came a tremendous jolt and the sound of people screaming. I clawed my fingers deep into the seat arm and braced my feet on the footrest to resist being thrown forward. Through the window I caught a brilliant flash of flames and smoke shooting into the night. My heart pounded wildly and I thought, *Please, Lord, be with us*, as we lurched and jerked, nosing downward until, with a final sickening shudder, everything was still.

Where were we? The superliner was dark inside and lodged at a strange angle. There were no lights—only the flickering orange glow of a fire somewhere up ahead. *Lord, don't let me panic.* I started to stand when a cry went up from the back of the compartment, "We're in water!" More people started yelling. Suddenly I realized I was standing in water nearly up to my knees. The stench of diesel fuel filled my head. I looked outside again. I noticed water leveling off several inches above the bottom of the window. The rubber seal was holding. But for how long?

"The water's deep back here!" a panicky voice called out. Drenched figures struggled forward in the faint light, pushing and stumbling. Moans filled the compartment. How many people were hurt? Were there any dead? *Dear God . . .* Then I heard a faint, choking call, "Help! Help!"

No one else seemed to hear. "Help!" the cry came again, fainter this time but still quite distinct. Adrenaline shot through me. "Help!" People were assisting the injured and answering their calls but no one seemed to hear this cry. It was so near! I had to do something.

I scanned the compartment. Through the dimness I saw a spot where there were no seats. Of course, the stairway! The plea came from that black, watery hole! I was sure of it. Amid all the groans and hollering, somehow I knew that spot was the source of the cry.

I grabbed a large man passing by in the aisle. "There's someone down there," I insisted, pointing. We stumbled over to the stairway and the man probed the water with his foot. Gripping the railing, he took a cautious step down and groped through the water. Nothing. He took another step down. Again he searched the oily water, his arm disappearing fully to his shoulder. I could see the muscles bulge in his neck. Then with a lunging heave he pulled up what looked like a mass of dripping rags from the hole. It was a young girl. He thrust the limp body into my arms.

She started coughing, gagging, and shivering violently. Thank God, she was alive! I swept away the thick, matted hair from her face. She couldn't have been older than twelve. As I placed her in a seat, word filtered back that someone had got an emergency window open. Then a steady, authoritative voice rang out, "Everybody stay put. We're lodged on some type of piling. Any sudden shift of weight and we might plunge all the way in."

People stayed calm and still. I saw couples holding hands and others comforting the injured. I could hear people praying quietly, and silently I joined in. But the little girl was straining her head and struggling, jerking her arms. "I can't walk," she gasped. "I use a wheelchair." I stroked and soothed her, wrapping her in my arms to keep her still. She wanted to know where her parents were. I tried to keep her quiet. Finally she put her head down on the tray table, exhausted.

The minutes ticked by. How much longer before the water came rushing in? Or the fire reached us? Then the news crackled through the car: "A boat's coming!" I leaned over to look out. A small skiff cutting through the fog, followed by another. Not enough for a major rescue. "Get the baby on first, the hurt, and the elderly," someone ahead ordered. People made way.

"This little girl can't walk," I announced, raising my arm. Quickly a man lifted her up and carried her to be put on a boat. *Dear God, keep her safe.* A minute later another announcement came: "If you can swim, you can take your chances in the water."

I can swim a little, I thought. *I might be able to make it.* I climbed forward. "Are you sure about this?" a man asked, no doubt noticing my age. I nodded. A pair of strong arms helped me through the window.

I felt the shock of water hitting my face as I went under. I came up saturated with diesel fuel, eyes burning. The taste in my mouth was dreadful. A piece of railroad tie floated by. I grabbed it, pushed away from the superliner with my feet and began kicking. Now I could see that only the upper compartment was above water level. *God, I don't know which way to go, but when you get me there, I will be sure to give you all the credit.*

In a few minutes I spotted powerful beams of light piercing the fog from shore. I kicked toward them. Finally I made it. When I was helped onto land, I glanced at my watch. It had stopped at 4:00 A.M.

From newspaper reports the next day I learned that a barge had hit and weakened the bridge over Bayou Canot minutes before the Sunset Limited came roaring through the night. The two engines and first four cars plunged into the bayou, located about twelve miles northeast of Mobile.

I also read about an eleven-year-old survivor named Andrea Chancey who had cerebral palsy. Studying a newspaper's diagram of the Superliner car I had been on, I saw that the lower level had a wheelcair-accessible section for disabled travelers. That's where Andrea and her parents must have been. Tragically, Andrea's parents perished. And though her memories of the crash are scant, she vaguely recalls being pushed upward to safety.

I thought of that small cry for help and what I had felt the Sunday before in church. Yes, we do have to listen carefully for the Lord's voice. Sometimes it comes in a call for help—a call that no one else can hear.

Be on your guard; stand firm in faith;
be men of courage; be strong.
—I CORINTHIANS 16:13

THE HARDEST BATTLE

JULIE WEST GARMON

The doctor had been very matter-of-fact after my ultrasound, but a certain sentence she said rewound in my mind and played over and over again: "Your baby's head is so low, I can't get accurate head measurements, but everything looks fine." I was thirty-two weeks pregnant and an earlier ultrasound at six weeks revealed my baby should be born May 28, 1989. Without asking any questions, I quickly left the doctor's office, and by the time I got into my car and started driving home, I knew a mighty battle had begun in my mind.

I tried to reassure myself that everything was fine. I told my husband, Rick, I was certain everything was okay. But since I had worked for a pediatric group before having children, I was familiar with a term that kept racing around in my mind. *Anencephaly*. "Anencephaly . . . a birth defect with the absence of some or most of the brain. Chance of occurrence one in one thousand." I spent hours secretly searching through medical books from the library. Everything I read fueled the fierce battle going on inside me. My suspicion was too agonizing to share with my doctors or even my husband. Some days the fear would advance unexpectedly and defeat any peace I'd tried to gain. Other days, fear hid quietly. But just as day always turns to night, fear returned to attack my thoughts.

Decorating the nursery happened in slow motion. . . . I had cute ideas, but when I went shopping, buying baby things felt oddly somber. Friends asked why I hadn't fixed up the room sooner. I pretended to be busy with my daughters, Jamie, eight, and Katie, six. I felt unattached to the baby furniture, like it belonged in a department store. Finally, as my due date came closer, Jamie and Katie helped me pick out a border with geese, hearts, and teddy bears. Rick insisted that this would finally be our boy so we painted the furniture red and the walls bright yellow. After we finished decorating, I looked slowly around the room. "There," I whispered to myself. "A happy, wonderful nursery and even more elaborate than the first two. Surely this means a perfect baby will grow up here." But my mind continued to battle.

Twelve days past my due date, contractions began at nine in the morning. At nine that night, we entered the hospital. Within an hour, and after four ultrasounds, I knew I was living out my nightmare. During the third ultrasound, I gravely commented to one of the doctors, "I know what you're looking for. You're trying to find the top of the baby's head. And you're thinking anencephaly." At last, I had spoken the words that had terrified me.

The doctors performing the scan stopped their silent motions. Finally one admitted, "You're right. We're ninety percent sure we're dealing with an anencephalic infant." It was as though I was locked into a horror movie and couldn't find the exit door. The labor room squeezed in on us. We were underwater with no oxygen. Rick held my hand tightly, "It'll be okay, Julie."

"No, you don't understand, Rick. The baby will live maybe hours, but not more than a few days. We won't be taking a baby home!" I had begun to speak in whispers.

When Rick understood what we were facing, he looked away. My eyes followed his. Outside the huge picture window, it was dark and raining. We cried in unison with the rain. *Will I always hate the rain? Will it always suffocate me like this?*

Gently, and very quietly, small bits of Scripture began to come to me like a floating life preserver in rushing water. I grabbed them desperately. "What time I am afraid I will trust in Thee [*Even in this, Lord*]. . . . Lean not to thine own understanding. . . . In all thy ways acknowledge him, and he will direct thy path."

God, this is unreal. People don't come to the hospital to have a baby and no one smiles. Why won't anyone smile at me? Someone please smile! Surely, I've been wrong all along. Surely the ten percent of error will win and my baby will be fine. The doctors communicated through a secret language, moving only their eyes. Mentally, I screamed, *Oh, let us go back home and begin all over again. We will start timing contractions and come back later. We want to come back another day. This can't be real.* The room felt incredibly heavy, almost like we were playing roles in a terribly sad movie. Even the rhythmic sounds of the baby's heart tones seemed to thump: *Bleakness . . . no hope . . . you were right all along. . . .*

But deep within me, wedged far below the crushing fear, a tiny speck of faith struggled relentlessly to emerge. Finally, I acknowledged the hope and decided: *God . . . I trust you, no matter what.*

Shortly after my epidural, a blank-faced nurse offered me something to relax me. "No thank you," I said. My voice surprised me. No longer a whisper. I wanted to use my thoughts to draw me closer to God. Within a few minutes my hard trembling stopped. Amazingly, I felt as though I were floating on a raft in the middle of a warm, still lake. "My God shall supply all your needs according to his riches in Christ Jesus." A new worry jabbed at me, like a boxer with renewed strength. . . . "What about Jamie and Katie? Rick, how will they understand this?" Especially Katie. She loved to go to doctor's appointments with me. I remembered how she smiled first with her huge brown eyes and then her mouth as she heard the heartbeat each time. And Jamie loved to kiss my big tummy goodnight every night.

"I'll tell them," Rick said confidently as he pulled on his familiar "Daddy green" scrub suit. Hospitals should offer another color scrub suit to men who were losing a baby. Rick looked out of place now, like he'd come dressed to a wedding in cut-off jeans. *Please go change clothes, Rick. You don't look right.*

We moved to the delivery room as if we were entering a dungeon. The delivery was long and difficult . . . like swimming across miles of endless ocean water. "When you go through the waters, I will be with you. . . . " Our son, Robert Clifford Garmon, was born at three-twenty in the morning on June 9, 1989. He lived for twenty-five minutes. After his birth, there were no triumphant, "It's a boy!" shouts. Total silence. Each person played their part in the painful, silent pantomime. *Somebody say something to us. Look at us. Stop looking away from me!* In the recovery room, I sobbed to Rick, "Why a son? Why did it have to be a son?" as though he knew a soothing answer.

I asked to see Robbie. Rick had examined him thoroughly just after he was born. Robbie had been carefully wrapped in a blue blanket and had on a little white cap. His face was very bruised from delivery, but perfect. His pug nose looked just like Katie's. He weighed just over six pounds. He came and left so quickly. *Hello, Robbie. Goodbye, Robbie.* Rick hurried home to take apart the nursery and make funeral plans. Then he came right back to the hospital for me. The doctors released me just nine hours after Robbie's birth.

Rick and I drove silently straight to my mother's house from the hospital. I practiced all the way to her house to see Jamie and Katie, blinking my eyes hard and opening them wide. Rick had explained about their little brother to them and told me they were doing fine. But I could picture their sad faces . . . and could feel their disappointment. We drove up the driveway and they ran down to us. They were smiling, each holding a box of Nerds candy. We held hands and went inside. My mother must have braided Katie's hair that morning. Her pigtails bounced as she jumped up next to me on the sofa and said right away, "If Robbie had lived we would have bought him a box of Nerds, but he's in heaven."

Jamie added, "Grady's probably holding him right now." (Grady is their name for my father, who died five years earlier.) "I'll bet Grady said, 'Here comes Robbie!'" They sat very close to me, smiling genuine smiles. *No bitterness! No anger! No complaints! Acceptance during a tragedy. Oh Lord, you are healing my broken-hearted children and are binding up their wounds. Thank you.*

My heart took a little longer to heal. Some days I felt strong, but grieving is tricky. . . . it sneaks up from behind and throws unexpected punches. The soft color of baby blue felt like a quick right jab to the jaw. . . . new babies, especially boys, could knock me down for a while. A week before Robbie was born, my grandmother raised her knowledgeable right eyebrow and gently offered me some advice. Her pointed words felt like an extra puzzle piece. . . . I tried turning them to every angle, but they didn't seem to fit. I hadn't asked for her help. Now her words slid easily into my heart: "The hardest battles are not fought in the battlefields, but in a mother's heart."

Two Augusts later, we went to a different hospital. No rain in sight that day . . . hot and steamy outside. As soon as I heard his bossy-sounding cry, I knew we had another son. Richard "Thomas" Garmon. As I watched Rick hold Thomas with both arms tucked around him, his hands gently cupping Thomas's perfectly formed head, a deep prayer of gratitude grew in my heart. . . . *O God, just like in 2 Chronicles, the people "cried out to God in battle, and he was entreated for them, because they trusted in him." Thank you . . . thank you. You were with me the whole time . . . even when I didn't understand. Even when it didn't make sense.*

The battle was finally over. God never loses.

Flowers grow out of dark moments.
—CORITA KENT

DEVASTATION AT DAWN

BRENDA HARVEY AS TOLD TO GLORIA CASSITY STARGEL

Six-twenty A.M. The alarm clock at our bedside jarred me half-awake. I reached over and hit the snooze control. *Ah! Thirty more minutes before I have to start my day.* In the distance I detected a roll of thunder. But last night's weather forecast for the Gainesville, Georgia, area had issued no severe-storm warnings, so I drifted back into a peaceful sleep. Beside me, my husband, Danny, never stirred.

Five months earlier we had completed the building of our home and moved in. For the first time, our sons, Chase, ten, and Tyler, twelve, had their own rooms and were feeling quite grown-up. Life was good. Curled up under a couple blankets on that morning of March 20, 1998, I was as oblivious to the outside world as a bear in hibernation.

6:34 A.M. "Mom . . . Dad . . ." I became aware of Chase standing in our bedroom door. " I think you need to wake up," he said.

I propped up on one elbow. I could see my younger son was visibly shaken. "What's wrong, Chase? You're never up this early."

"Something's not right, Mom. And the lights just went out."

Something's not right, I realized with a start. *The air feels strange.* Just then I heard it! Not a freight-train sound, but that of a monster thunder roll that never let up. And it was getting closer. And closer. There was no doubt. *Tornado!* Fear catapulted me into action. I shook my husband awake. "Danny! Danny! Hurry!"

"Get to the basement, quick!" Danny shouted as he yanked on a pair of pants. I grabbed a robe and raced behind Chase toward the basement stairs. Passing through the kitchen, I saw something I never want to see again—the walls and doors bulged outward. Through the windows, a gray mass swirled wildly, a mass so thick I could not see the porch railings.

About the same moment, our fire alarm shrilled into action. "Fire! Leave house immediately!" The outside horn sounded full blast, competing with the horror of the twister's increasing roar.

Just then a deadly calm settled over everything—a calm like nothing I'd ever experienced. Not a sound could be heard, except the intermittent signal from our smoke alarm. *Dear God in heaven, help us!*

"Go on down, Chase!" I flew into Tyler's room. His bed was empty. At the head of the stairs, I yelled, "Tyler, are you down there?" I heard a very frightened, "Yes."

"Both of you?"

"Yes."

"Hurry, Danny, hurry!" I hollered toward the other end of the house, knowing now that a killer storm had us in its sights. We were about to take a direct hit. "Danny!" The tornado-created vacuum blocked my voice mere inches from my face. The house moaned. Starting down the steps, on the third one I hesitated. Never have I been so torn: *Where is Danny? What to do? I need to be with the children. But I can't leave him up here!*

Seconds later, the choice was made for me.

6:35 A.M. The roar was upon us. Unleashed fury struck full force at two hundred miles an hour, an F4 tornado. Terrified, I gripped the handrail as I shouted for Danny. But now the sound was swallowed up in ear-splitting sounds, sounds too horrible to believe, as our home literally exploded around me. Glass shattered, wood splintered, metal crumpled, roofing ripped, insulation shredded, rafters fell, fireplace rocks crashed. Unidentified objects became wild missiles. The odor of Sheetrock dust overwhelmed the senses as walls and ceilings were pulverized. The shrieking wind was deafening.

One wall beside me tore away. I was jerked first one way, then another. Shards of glass and bits of concrete block mixed with red mud bombarded me from all sides. Out of the corner of my eye I spotted a huge black thing flying through the air just before it hit me in the head. The force sent me careening down the stairs, my bare toes doubling under. Everything went black for a few seconds. Yet my subconscious kept saying, *The children. You've got to stay alert for the children.*

Suddenly, it was over, just as quickly as it began. Another eerie quiet descended. Not a sound. No birds. No nothing. I forced my eyes open. Chase and Tyler stood right where they started, except soaking wet. The vacuum had pulled all the water out of the downstairs commode and drenched them with it. "Are you both okay?" "Yes," they answered shakily, about to cry, "but where is Daddy?" *Danny! Oh, Lord, is he dead?* "You boys stay here." I didn't want them to see what I feared I'd find.

The stairs were blocked with debris. I pushed aside boards, being careful of protruding nails, and lifted what appeared to be part of a door. With great effort I made it to the top. I could not believe my eyes. Without warning—in fifteen seconds of utter devastation—our new home was no more. The only thing not demolished was the back wall of our breakfast room, complete with three unbroken windows. On the other side of that room, where the laundry area used to be, Danny's blue and white Ford pickup and our black Jimmy had been blown in from the garage. Both were totaled.

I called out a tentative, "Danny?"

"Brenda?"

"Danny!" Could this be true? "Danny, where are you? Are you hurt?" Just then I saw him crawling out over the truck. I started toward him.

"No, Brenda, don't come this way! Too much glass. And hot wires. Are the boys safe?"

"Yes, downstairs."

"Go back with them and come out the basement door."

We met in the front yard, ecstatic to be alive and together. Standing there shivering in our bare feet, we were too much in shock to comprehend what we were seeing. Everything we had was gone. We didn't even own a toothbrush. But we had each other and that is what really mattered. *Thank you, God. Thank you.*

When we calmed down a bit I had to know, "Where were you, Danny? Why didn't you come on right behind us?"

"You won't believe this," he said. "I stopped to quiet the smoke alarm. I was afraid it would disturb the neighbors."

"Danny, you could have gotten us both killed!"

"Don't I know it. I guess I was still half asleep and not thinking clearly. But when the back door flew off beside me, I knew I had waited too long. I just fell down, face-first, right where I was. Soon a piece of Sheetrock fell on top of me, protecting me somewhat. And now that I see where my truck ended up, I know it protected me as well."

The room where Danny fell flat happened to be the breakfast room, the one with the only wall still intact. He suffered only minor cuts and bruises. My scalp was embedded with concrete-block chips and glass shards, and my hair—encrusted with red mud—stuck straight out. At the hospital, x-rays ruled out a concussion or broken toe. When I got back, Danny was standing outside the ruins holding a crumpled birdcage. "Oh, no. Chipper!" Our bright yellow parakeet's cage had been by the fireplace in the living room. We abandoned hope of ever seeing him again.

Two days later, Danny and Tyler were cleaning up the rubble when they heard a faint chirp. They looked at each other. You don't think . . . ? They began moving a pile of fireplace rocks and there, buried under one, lay a cold, hungry, scared but otherwise unhurt Chipper.

The boys' beds were never found but part of ours landed on top of my sister's house, half a mile away. Our fully-stocked camper, which had been parked on the right side of the house, ended up in a field on the other side. That is, the metal frame did—stripped bare. We discovered in our basement the object that hit me on the head—the inner drum of our neighbor's washing machine.

Later, when we could discuss things rationally, I asked Chase, "Honey, what woke you that morning? Whatever it was saved our lives."

Chase hesitated a moment. "I didn't know how to tell you, " he started. "I can't say for sure what woke me the first time, but I got up and looked out the window, then went back to bed. That's when it happened. Something—or someone—moved a hand across the back of my hair. I knew I was supposed to come wake you." He gave me a look which said, *You're not going to believe this*. "Mom, it was my guardian angel. I didn't see her but I know it was."

"Oh, yes, Chase, I believe you," I said as I grabbed him in a bear hug, remembering that within scant moments of his leaving his room, that room was obliterated. As was Tyler's room—and ours!

Without warning? It appears that we got an advance warning after all. A warning from Chase's guardian angel.

Skeptics might say static electricity caused Chase's hair to stand on end. I don't worry about that, though. It is enough that in the midst of the storm, God brought us through. And I know now that when future storms rage about me—which they will, of one kind or another—I can continue to rest in his care—safe and secure.

The
Renewal
of Faith

God enters by a private door into every individual.
—RALPH WALDO EMERSON

ONE SIMPLE WORD FROM GOD

MARION BOND WEST

The night before Jerry's brain surgery were the most horrible hours of my life. I'd had a cot set up in the hospital room beside my husband of almost twenty-five years, but I could not sleep. I could feel fear moving around inside me, slowly but forcefully, like a full-term baby.

All my life I'd been hounded by fear—thoughts beginning with the words "What if . . .?" *What if Jerry loses his job? What if one of the children has an accident?*

Now the what-ifs stretched and kicked and elbowed me. *What if it's malignant? What if they can't get it all? What if Jerry dies? What if I have to watch him suffer for months and months?*

I knew Scripture. I knew how to pray. I'd told others in similar situations, "Just stand on the Word. Jesus is the healer." Now there was no room in me for anything but the what-ifs.

Seven A.M.: nurses woke Jerry to prep him. He'd slept all night without even a sleeping pill, and soon he had the staff laughing at his jokes. I heard the stretcher wheels coming down the hall. Jerry opened his arms and we hugged hard. As they rolled him away, I clung to his hand and walked alongside him to the elevator. *Jerry, oh Jerry, you are part of me. The best part. I'm having brain surgery too. Only they aren't putting me to sleep.*

The waiting room was crowded with family and friends and people from Jerry's office. Our married daughter was there with her husband. Our twenty-year-old daughter, Jennifer. Our fourteen-year-old twin sons. All the people dearest to me in the world . . . except one.

And that one was strong, healthy, athletic! Jerry was forty-seven and had never been sick a day in his life.

I asked if I could see the room in the intensive care unit where they'd bring him after the operation. "Of course," the nurse smiled. Too nice. Everyone was being too nice.

I knelt down by the bed. Three hot tears slid down my face and spotted the sterile covers. "Please, God, I'll do anything! Just let him be all right."

But Jerry was not all right. The tumor was highly malignant, and doctors were able to remove only part of it. They gave him only months to live.

In the ICU cubicle Jerry and I talked about Jesus the healer, and all the while I was silently telling God I cannot live without him. Whenever Jerry had a business trip, he'd wait until the last moment to tell me. I always hit rock bottom when I knew he had to be gone, even for one night. *I can't. You need to understand that, God. I grew up without a daddy, and I can't grow old without a husband.*

Already the fear of our house without Jerry had taken hold of me, and I knew I couldn't go home that night. I couldn't turn into our driveway or walk up the steps past the roses Jerry had planted. Friends had to take me and the two boys to their house that night. I realized I was walking a beaten, humble walk, and I'd started to whisper when I talked.

Had I but known it, I had come to the most enviable place any human being can reach. Because I was defeated and desperate, I was only a step away from the unimaginable joy of "Nevertheless" living. But I didn't know it, and it would be seven devastating months before I took that step.

Jerry took the step right away. He reacted to the bad news from the doctors by drawing even closer to God. And to me. He came home five days after his surgery able to express his love as never before. The intimacy, the deep sharing, for which I'd begged him over the years, he gave me now in abundance.

Which only increased my anguish. Every evening about six I became almost physically sick. That was when I'd been accustomed to sit in a chair by the window and watch for his car—a habit I had formed in childhood when I watched for Mother to come home from work.

Now, although Jerry was right there at home, I would go into the living room at six o'clock and look out, hurting, terrified. The cars moving past all had husbands in them. *I can't live for my children*, I'd tell God. *Jerry is my world. I'm sorry. I know that's not right, but he is.*

It wasn't exactly like praying. God seemed far away. The what-ifs were the only voices I could hear.

Christmas was awful. I'd stand in line at the drugstore to get a prescription filled for Jerry, while "Joy to the World" piped through the air and wives talked about what they were getting their husbands. *Only four months ago*, I thought, *I was like these women. Illness was foreign to us. Oh, God, why can't we go back?*

But there was no going back. By March Jerry had headaches almost continuously. I chased after every cancer treatment I heard of. I read about a new "wonder" drug and got some of it shipped to us. "The patient's wife," the doctor wrote in a report I saw later, "is phoning medical centers all over the country. She is, of course, desperate."

That desperation, had I but known it, meant that I was on the royal highway to "Nevertheless" living.

We had set up a hospital bed in the recreation room downstairs. One evening as Jerry was undressing there, he toppled over backward. He fell stiff like a store mannequin, eyes wide open. With the help of Jennifer and the boys, I got him into the car and to the hospital, where they discovered brain swelling.

For the next three days I drove despairingly back and forth between the house and the hospital. And it was on one of these trips, on a spring evening, May 11, 1983, that God did something in my life that I cannot understand, let alone explain. The greatest change, the greatest miracle, of my life occurred—"Nevertheless" living began.

The brain swelling had gone down some and Jerry was to go home next day. The sun was setting as I drove home. I'd come to hate sunsets. *You knew I didn't want to be alone, God. You knew that.*

And suddenly—it was as though the sun's rays came right inside the car. Everything around me was golden. I felt golden, too. And not at all alone. Something very close to joy seemed to have entered the car with me. For a moment I wondered if the car was just going to float up off the highway.

Then into that golden silence, God spoke a word. That was all. One word. I knew it was from Scripture, but it wasn't even a verse. It was a single word.

Nevertheless.

I knew it had to be a special word, though I didn't yet know it would become a lifestyle. I was sure only that it was a kind of promise. It was even a powerful little phrase: *never the less.*

Never the less with God, no matter what. Always the most. Though I was alone in this automobile, nevertheless God himself was right here beside me. Though doctors pronounced Jerry incurable, nevertheless he would be gloriously healed. Perhaps not here on earth as we had all prayed. If Jerry's physical body should die, nevertheless he would go on living in another, greater dimension.

I gazed out the window at the glorious sunset. "Thank you," I whispered.

"What if you're losing your mind?" It was the voice of fear—fear that had been with me so long that even in this radiant moment it could bully and bluster. "What if you've finally flipped under the pressure?"

I am not the God of What-If, I heard in the golden twilight. *I am the God of Nevertheless.* It was the moment when I first spoke aloud my new word: "Nevertheless," I told the fear-voice, "I know that this is real."

Fear was silent.

The next morning I put on my best clothes when I went to bring Jerry home. No one, except Jerry, understood my overnight change, but it didn't matter. Somehow it didn't even seem to matter that I might be left alone, a widow. I was excited for Jerry.

As his body grew thinner and weaker and fear renewed its attacks, "nevertheless" could always send it scurrying. I began to research this word in the Bible, wondering why no one had ever told me about this principle before. I found it used more than ninety times, always with tremendous power:

"I said in my haste, I am cut off from before thine eyes: nevertheless thou heardest the voice of my supplications" (Psalm 31:22).

"Master, we have toiled all the night, and have taken nothing: nevertheless at thy word I will let down the net" (Luke 5:5).

"I am crucified with Christ: nevertheless I live" (Galatians 2:20).

I engaged two Christian nurses and knew I could keep Jerry at home until the end, though doctors told me no one keeps a brain tumor patient at home. As his abilities declined, Jerry's love for God grew to unbelievable proportions. I would sit beside him on the bed and we would pray and laugh and listen to praise music on the phonograph.

July 16 was a Saturday. Jerry's breathing was labored, and fear tried again. "Your husband is dying."

"Nevertheless," I shot back, "God is in control. This is the recreation room."

Knowing that the end was close, nevertheless about 11:30 that night I lay down on the sofa. Here was the what-if I'd been so terrified of. Now that it was actually happening, I was drowsy, relaxed. . . .

At 12:45 A.M. Sunday morning Jennifer called, "Come quick!" When I got there, just two steps, it was over. Jerry's form, his earthsuit, didn't seem to be a big deal. My husband wasn't here anymore. He was in glory—running, leaping, more whole than ever before.

I miss him dreadfully, of course. Nor has it been easy being a single parent, or learning all the things I had to learn—how to get the house painted, how to fill out insurance forms. Nevertheless I managed—and each time the what-ifs were a little easier to silence.

On my birthday, a year after Jerry died, I went out to the backyard just as the sun was rising. The day was cool and new and smelled like hope. "Thank you, Father, for today. Thank you that I'm not afraid of the future. Oh, I know there's plenty I could be worrying about. Nevertheless you are in charge."

The dew shone so bright on the grass that I thought, *This could well be the most joyful day of my life so far.* . . .

Your faith is what you believe, not what you know.
—JOHN LANCASTER SPALDING

VISITATION

JOHN SHERRILL

I was in an upbeat mood that morning in 1959, striding uptown for a follow-up visit at my doctor's. I'd been coming to Daniel Catlin's office every month since an operation two years earlier for melanoma, a particularly vicious form of cancer. Always before it was the same: The surgeon's skilled fingers running down my neck, the pat on the back. "See you in a month."

But not that day. This time Dr. Catlin's fingers stopped, prodded, worked a long time. He shook his head. When I left I was scheduled for surgery at New York's Memorial Hospital the following day.

What a difference in a spring morning! I walked back down the same street in the same sunshine, but now a cold, light-headed fear walked with me. I was not expected to live beyond three months.

Tib and I were having coffee the next morning after a sleepless night when the telephone rang. It was our neighbor, Catherine Marshall LeSourd. "John," she said, "could you and Tib drive over? I've heard the news and there's something I've got to ask you." Catherine met us at the door dressed in a housecoat, wearing neither makeup nor smile. She led us into the family room, shut the door and, without polite talk, began.

"First of all I want to say that I know it's presumptuous to ask you about your religious life. I have no right to assume that it lacks anything."

I looked at Tib: she sat still as a rock.

"John," said Catherine, "Do you believe that Jesus was God?"

It was the last question I'd expected. I'd supposed she'd have something to say about God's power to heal, or the crisis I faced. But she'd put the question to me, so I considered it. Tib and I were Christians, certainly, in the sense that we attended various churches off and on, and sent our three children to Sunday school. Still, I had never come to grips with this very question: Was Jesus of Nazareth in fact God? And now, when I tried to do so, there were mountains of logic in the way. I started to map them for Catherine, but she stopped me.

"You're trying to arrive at faith through your mind, John," she said. "It simply can't be done that way. It's one of the peculiarities of Christianity," she went on, "that you have to do something you don't understand before you can understand. And it's this I'm hoping for you today—that without knowing why, against all logic, you say yes to Christ."

There was silence in the room and I had a sudden desire to do precisely what Catherine was suggesting. Yet I had reservations. The biggest of all, I stated frankly: It didn't seem right to shy away from Christ all these years and then come running when I had my back to the wall.

"John," said Catherine almost in a whisper, "that's pride. You want to come to God your way. As you will. When you will. Maybe God wants you now, without a shred to recommend you."

We talked for perhaps a half hour more. When Tib and I left, I still had not brought myself to take the step that was apparently all-crucial. A few moments later, however, as we drove past a telephone pole on Millwood Road, a pole that I can point out to this day, I turned to Tib.

"What do they call it? A leap of faith? All right, I'm going to make the leap: I believe that Jesus was God."

It was a cold-blooded laying down of my sense of what was logical, quite without emotional conviction. And with it went something that was essentially "me." All the bundle of self-consciousness that we call our ego seemed to dissolve in this decision. It was amazing how much it hurt. But when this thing was dead and quiet finally, and I had blurted out my simple statement of belief, there was room for something new and altogether mysterious.

Millwood Road was the route to St. Mark's Episcopal Church in Mount Kisco, New York, where Tib and I had attended services for the past several months. We headed there now. The gray stone church offered solidity, permanence. And though the rector, Marc Hall, a retired Navy officer, was new to the priesthood, to a Christian five minutes old he was a veteran of the faith.

To our relief Marc was in. He stood up, unwinding his angular frame from behind his desk, and extended a huge hand. I told him I was entering Memorial Hospital that afternoon for surgery the next day and asked if the church had prayers for a situation like mine.

Marc reached for *The Book of Common Prayer*. "I know there are. . . . " As he thumbed the pages, I had the sense that he felt as shy hearing my request as I'd been in making it. "Ah, here we are. Shall we go into the chapel?"

Midmorning light streamed through Tiffany windows into the Chapel of the Resurrection. Holding the prayer book, Marc stepped behind the altar before him on the needlepoint cushion.

Marc plunged into the prayer. Certain words stood out: "I lay my hand upon thee . . . beseeching the mercy of our Lord Jesus Christ. . . . " Marc hesitated, then I felt one of those big hands on my head. "That all thy pain and sickness of body being put to flight, the blessing of health may be restored unto thee."

At that moment I felt a sudden rush of heat. Marc's hand was burning! The heat coursed down the side of my head and settled in my neck just where the surgeon's fingers had stopped the day before. Marc finished the prayer in a choked voice. I began to cry. So did Tib. The heat in Marc's hand burned, scorched, singeing my neck.

I heard Marc close the book. Tib and I stood up. The three of us stood blinking at each other, stunned, tearful, awed, embarrassed. Baffled by what had taken place. Quite unready to talk about it.

Four hours later Tib accompanied me as I checked into Memorial Hospital. That evening Dr. Catlin stopped by my bedside, trailed by half a dozen young physicians. "Melanoma," he told them, looking at his chart. He ran his free hand down the side of my neck. A puzzled look spread across his face. He put down his chart and felt my neck now with both hands, pursed his lips, felt again. With the young doctors in tow, he retreated to the hall where I heard, " . . . better go in anyhow."

What was happening? And why was I curiously uninterested? It was as if in some secret and undefined part of myself I knew that no matter how this operation turned out, it was only an inconvenience in an existence that was new and strange and quite independent of surgeons and hospitals, illness and recovery.

Early the next morning orderlies wheeled me into the operating room. I remember the bright lights overhead, and the green-masked face of Dr. Catlin looking down at me.

It seemed only an instant later that I was awake again, in a room I had never seen before. It was dark outside the window—but I'd gone into the operating room at eight in the morning. Why had it taken so long? Plastic tubes protruded from both sides of my chest, and from a hole in my throat. I could hear machines gurgling. And there was pain. The worst I had ever known.

In the morning I woke up in yet another room. The tubes were still in my chest and throat, machines still bubbled away. But there was wonderful news. Dr. Catlin leaned over the bed: "You're doing fine. There was some trouble on the operating table. Your lungs collapsed. Tracheotomy. The tumor in your neck, though . . ." The same puzzled look as when he'd spoken to the young doctors. "I didn't find it. Just a little dried-up pea, more like a cinder."

For the rest of that day I lay there in pain, aware of an occasional visit from Tib or the doctor, trying to take in the fact that a healing miracle could take place through a prayer in a suburban church.

That night I became more aware of the two other patients in the room. One, an older man, coughed almost constantly. The other, a teenager just down from Recovery, moaned in pain. Despite my embryonic faith I tried praying for them, but the coughing and the moans continued.

In the middle of the night I was awake suddenly. Fully awake. A dim yellow light came in from the hall; a nurse passed the door on rubbersoled shoes. Both of my roommates were restless.

Then a light came through the outer wall of the hospital. It was simply there, as abruptly as I'd awakened. It was different from the light coming through the door, warmer, yet more intense, with—indescribably—a center of awareness. I was awed, but not at all afraid.

"Christ?" I said.

The light moved. Rather, it was immediately closer to me. I thought for a moment that the pain beneath my bandages was going away, but it did not. Something had changed, though. Despite the pain, I felt as if I were bursting with health.

My roommates were still tossing, still coughing and groaning. "Christ," I said, "would you help that boy?" The light did not leave me, but in some strange way it was also now at the bedside of the teenager. A little "Ohhh . . ." came from him and he was silent.

"And my other friend?" The light was instantly centered on the bed of the old man who was in the midst of another coughing spasm. The coughing stopped.

And the light was gone.

I lifted my head from the pillow and searched the room but there was only the yellow light from the hall. A car honked outside in the night. The machines behind my bed gurgled. Everything was as it had been. Except that, lying in a bed in Memorial Hospital, with bandages around my neck and chest, with pain slicing through me, I was filled with a sense of well-being such as I had never known. I cried for a long time, out of joy.

I stayed awake until dawn. All the while my two roommates slept quietly.

I was out of the hospital a full week earlier than expected, so rapidly did my body mend. For several days afterward I tried to tell Tib about the encounter in the hospital, but every time I opened my mouth I felt tears well up. I knew that if I said one word I'd be weeping like a child. It was only when I decided that Tib would have to know about the experience, tears or no, that I managed to get it out.

"Do you think it was a dream?" I asked.

"I don't believe a dream could affect you this way."

"Neither do I."

Before that experience, I had been given three months to live. Since that day, to my surprise, a reality far more engrossing than physical survival has occupied my mind: the reality of Jesus Christ, whose light has shaped my life ever since—as vivid, mysterious, and joy-filled today as it was in that predawn hour so many years ago.

If ye have faith as a grain of mustard seed, ye shall say unto this mountain, Remove hence to yonder place; and it shall remove; and nothing shall be impossible unto you.

—MATTHEW 17:20B

A SPROUTING OF FAITH

H. J. DUFFY

When my sister Eleanor was in the third grade, she memorized Matthew 17:20, about faith "the size of a mustard seed." Ellie liked the idea of relocating mountains. One night at dinner, she speared a lima bean with her fork, lifted it toward her mouth and stared at it, her eyes dark enough to entertain magic or sadness. My eyes were always a simple blue.

"What's the matter, Eleanor?" Mom asked.

"If I had the faith of a lima bean," Ellie said slowly, "I could do anything." Two years younger than Eleanor, I already believed she could.

That summer, Ellie became a magician. We made her a black cape to wear over her favorite overalls. Ellie had perfect posture, while I slumped, never quite comfortable with my height.

I was the magician's assistant. Eleanor gave me a suit, a piecemeal of Dad's wardrobe, garlands to enhance our costumes. Ellie wanted to drape tree lights around my shoulders for our grand finale, but Mom drew the line at electricity.

One of my jobs was procuring props. I had to ask Dad for spare change to replace the nickels and dimes we lost practicing our coin trick. "I don't know about this magic stuff, Joe," Dad said, handing me nickels. "Just remember the biggest magic trick is nothing compared to God's tiniest miracle."

"I'll remember," I promised, never guessing how badly I'd come to need a miracle for my sister, the magician.

Ellie traded in her magic tricks for soft-lead pencils, charcoals, and watercolors. By her thirteenth birthday, every square inch of blank paper seemed rich with promise in my sister's hands. Ellie painted scenery for the Christmas program the next year. Her star of Bethlehem would have led the most doubtful wise man straight toward Jesus.

Then Eleanor began to change. She wouldn't paint or draw for days at a time. She stayed in her room, refusing to talk to anybody. Mom said Ellie was having growing pains on the inside. The spells lasted only a few days, then Eleanor would be her old self. We got used to the rhythms of my sister's emotions.

All through high school, her moods were like high and low tides. I was more like sand, shifting and resetting and waiting.

On her good days, certain things still held magic for Ellie. One night the summer before she left for college, we decided to sleep out in the back field. The moon was as narrow as a thumbnail clipping when Eleanor grabbed my dad's old kerosene lantern and I followed her, carrying pillows and Hershey bars and our old transistor radio.

We hung the lantern on a lonely fencepost, climbing into our sleeping bags right away even though it wasn't cold. Eleanor emptied her overall pockets of the stuff she'd collected that day. Mom said Ellie was a natural-born scavenger, but I understood something about my sister that no one else seemed to. Ellie slipped colors and shapes into her pockets, and carried their secrets for days. They solved a piece of some mystery for her.

Eleanor fished a set of copper measuring spoons from her pocket and dangled them between us. "Mom was looking for these this morning," I said. Ellie grinned, stacking a couple of pillows together and leaning back. "She probably just wanted to measure something with them." She held the spoons up overhead and studied each one separately, tracing the curves with her fingers.

I settled down beside my sister, trying to see what she saw. "What are you doing?"

"Trying to find the right one." She compared two. "I think it's this one. Turn the lantern down, Joe," she whispered.

I scooted out of my sleeping bag and crawled toward the light.

"Not so dark you can't see me," Eleanor said.

I dimmed the lantern, then moved back beside my sister. "I can see you."

"Remember when we were little and we pretended Mom's measuring spoons were really a ring of keys that turned on our tricycles?"

I nodded. I'd forgotten, but I believed Eleanor. My sister pointed toward heaven. "I used to think the stars were tiny silver tacks to hold up secret messages from God."

I liked the sound of Ellie's voice and the way the lantern light stuttered across her face when the breeze picked up. I squinted up at the sky. I tried imagining it as a huge bulletin board, and I scanned it for a message with my name on it.

"Maybe the sky is a door and the moon is a keyhole." Eleanor held the spoon high and turned it slowly. "This spoon could unlock the whole sky. It fits." She studied me. "We knew the spoons were keys, but we forgot."

"You didn't," I whispered.

"Sometimes I forget everything, even colors," Eleanor said softly. Then she asked me to turn the lantern off. Ellie was quiet for so long, I started to drift off to the lullaby of breezes through the tall grass. "Sometimes I have to name colors, just to remind myself the world isn't all gray," Ellie said. Then in a whisper, "Cyan, turquoise, magenta, slate, aqua, tangerine, emerald, quince, tyrian . . ." I fell asleep to my sister's words, quick, crooked brush strokes across my pale heart.

Eleanor had been away at college a few weeks when her roommate called. Ellie had stopped going to classes. She didn't paint or draw, and she wouldn't talk to anyone. Dad drove over and brought Ellie home.

The next few days were doctor visits, counseling sessions, and my parents' late-night whispers. One night, long after I should have been asleep, I stood in the hallway listening to my parents fight in the kitchen. "The doctor and the psychologist both agree," Mom said. "They think Eleanor has a biochemical problem. Dr. Stephens thinks an antidepressant might really help."

"We'll take her to another doctor," Dad said.

"Please, Harvey? At least consider it."

"You know how I feel about that." My father's voice was emphatic.

"I know you love Eleanor," Mom whispered. "Please, Harvey, at least talk to the doctor." I couldn't breathe, with my mother's voice making the air so thick and sad, so I went down the hall to bed.

Everybody at church prayed for my sister. I prayed hard for Eleanor, too, though I wasn't sure what to ask for. Some nights, I'd be in bed, listening to the quiet sadness of our house, and I'd think if I could just figure out the right words to say to God we'd all be OK again.

Ellie tried going to church with us. I was grateful for the way the congregation embraced Ellie so gently and quietly. She smiled and seemed really to try to make conversation, but on the way home in the car she closed her eyes and pressed her forehead into the passenger window. "Everyone was so nice . . . but my heart is so tired," she said, and my mother started to cry.

Not long after that, Ellie stopped coming out of her room during the day. Then she wouldn't get dressed. Within a few weeks she was spending all day in bed, pulling herself deeper under the covers, her old blue bedspread like a tide drawn slowly away from the shore but not returning.

Ellie's eyes were puffy almost every morning when I'd go in to tell her goodbye on my way to school. One Saturday, I brought her a piece of toast and some pineapple juice, her favorite. I sat on the edge of her bed like company, not knowing what to say.

Finally Eleanor took a sip of the juice. "I miss the colors," she said, her voice trembling. "Everything looks gray, like old pavement."

"Don't be scared," I told her, because I was.

That night, Daddy finally agreed to the medication but my sister refused. Ellie said she didn't need pills, just time. Mom kept at her until she decided the arguments were just making Eleanor worse. I didn't know what to say. I just knew my sister was in trouble.

Eleanor hadn't left her bed in six days the night I heard her sobbing. I climbed out of bed and stood just inside my open door. I'd been afraid to close my door at night since Ellie had gotten so bad. I closed my eyes and heard my mother's voice, so soft I followed it.

Mom was on the edge of my sister's bed. Ellie leaned across her, my mother gathering as much of my sister into her lap as she could. She rocked Ellie back and forth. "Nothing can separate us from the love of God, Eleanor." Mom's voice was swollen with tears. She repeated the same thing over and over. Ellie just sobbed, clinging to Mom.

Sometimes people repeat things because they don't really believe what they're saying, but Mom believed what she told Eleanor. Those words gave her heart enough weight to anchor my sister.

The next morning, Eleanor was curled in the middle of her bed asleep. She looked small and sinking, like an island being quietly swallowed. I tiptoed in and knelt beside my sister's bed. Eleanor opened her eyes and I knew right then that the sadness was inside her, an illness like the doctor told Mom. I knew, because Ellie didn't need a minute to wake up to remember her hurt. This sadness remembered itself. "It's bad, Joe," Eleanor whispered.

"Please try the medicine, Eleanor. It might help."

"I don't have any faith in pills."

I'd studied the bottle of tiny, deep green pills, wondering how something so small could help such huge pain. "You only have to swallow them. You have faith in God."

"I don't think I have enough faith left."

"Not even a lima bean's worth?" I tried to smile.

Eleanor shook her head, her eyes watery, "I'm too tired."

I didn't know what to say. My eyes searched Eleanor's room. All the magic tricks had become as useless as burnt-out sparklers, and the colors had been put away. Then I noticed a slender, black, felt-tipped marker lying on Ellie's desk. I stood and picked up the pen, crossing the room to the farthest yellow wall. I made a tiny mark somewhere near the center.

"What are you doing?"

"Drawing you a mustard seed."

"I can't see it."

"You're just too far away right now." I put the marker back on Ellie's desk. "I promise you it's there."

It took a lot of convincing and another conference with Dr. Stephens to get Ellie on the medication. She was afraid it wouldn't work, afraid she wouldn't be able to paint anything, afraid of losing herself. I was a little scared, too. I didn't want Eleanor to forget her own magic. At first, Ellie still slept a lot. The doctor had warned us the meditation might make her groggy for a while. Then one afternoon I came home and heard my sister moving around in her room. "I think Ellie's up," I told Mom.

"I know." Mom touched my shoulder. "I think she's better, Joe." Hope ached in her voice.

The following Saturday, I woke early. The house was quiet. Ellie's door was ajar so I peeked in. She was standing across the room, painting on the farthest, window-less wall. I watched as a tangle of mint-green vines and leaves grew slowly from her paintbrush. Then I slipped back out into the hall.

Later that week, Eleanor started eating dinner with us again. When Daddy said grace, he thanked God for "all those present at our table."

I said "Amen" in two drawn-out syllables, like a TV preacher, and Ellie laughed.

I don't know when Ellie's wall began to bloom. I don't know if the purple flowers or the yellow or the blue came first. By the time I saw it, the wall was a jungle of bright blooms and hopeful buds. Eleanor was asleep when I crept in to get a better look.

Ellie's mural was like one of those hidden picture puzzles we used to find in our Sunday school newsletters. You had to look at them a new way every time to find the fishing net or disciple's sandal or wayward sheep.

I didn't see Ellie and me until my focus shifted a little. Then I saw our shy faces back in the leaves. Our fingers tangled like twigs, through blue and orange and pur-ple flowers. My eyes traced emerald vines trailing down and around our shins like Maypole streamers. Ellie and I stood barefoot, our feet tangled together with lima beans sprouting everywhere.

It is the easiest thing in the world to obey God when he commands us to do what we like. . . . The real victory of faith is to trust God in the dark. . . .

—T. L. CUYLER

HIS UNFAILING LOVE

MARY ALICE BAUMGARDNER

I was with Mom and Dad when they went to the oncologist for her follow-up visit. He asked her what was 97 from 100.

Mom grinned and said, "103?"

"You never were any good in math, Mom," I teased.

I refused to look down at the situation. I had to keep my sight on the Lord. I could not, would not, look at the circumstances. For I knew if I did, fear would creep in and undermine my faith.

In February 1977, Mother had been diagnosed with a malignant tumor between her lungs that had spread to her brain. Doctors at The Hershey Medical Center gave her six months to live and said she would never recover any of the skills she had lost. Cobalt treatments might stop the rapid growth of the tumor. Chemotherapy was ruled out.

And so my father, brother, sister, and I sought the help of the Divine Physician. On Palm Sunday, two days after her last cobalt treatment, we helped Mother out of bed and took her to a healing service at Trinity Lutheran Church in Hagerstown, Maryland. Later, she told us that she knew "something happened" when Pastor Norris Wogan prayed for her.

We saw no immediate results. But we believed God would heal her.

Mother phoned me in June to report that the chest x-ray showed "no signs of any tumor"!

In July, she called to say that her CAT scan showed no evidence of any brain tumor. "The doctor said it has just 'melted away.' Honey," she said, "God has healed me!"

I was not surprised that Jesus had healed my mother, because I truly believed he would. But I was absolutely overwhelmed that God's healing touch had seemingly crossed the ages. It was as if he were right beside us. As I read the Bible, his words leaped from the pages into my heart. I felt so blessed, so very grateful to him.

Mother, whose "lost skills would never return," according to the doctors, passed the written driver's exam for her Pennsylvania license. She spoke at many churches, sharing her story, giving praise and glory to Jesus for healing her. And, yes, she would laugh and tell me what 97 from 100 was . . . the correct answer!

However, after two years, symptoms began to return, and gradually Mom became mute. The doctors could find no explanation, nor could the clergy, nor could we. No longer able to walk or take care of herself, she spent the last year of her life in a nursing home. I often visited her and would read the Bible to her. Sometimes I would prop her up in a wheelchair and take her to the community room, where I played the piano and sang the hymns we loved.

I could not understand what had happened. I prayed, "Dear Lord, if you are ready to take Mom home to heaven, please let me know." But my faith continued to be strong that she would be healed again. I could not grieve over the circumstances because I could picture the day when she would be well and all this would be like a bad dream.

I thanked Jesus for being with us. I was joyful even in those darkest of days. I trusted him.

Mother had been in the nursing home nearly a year. She had become totally mute and unresponsive. On February 20, 1980, she died.

As we were getting things together for her funeral, Dad opened her dresser drawer and discovered a piece of paper on top of her lingerie. All year, he had been in and out of that dresser drawer, taking things to her in the nursing home. No paper was there before. On it, written in Mother's perfect handwriting, was a message: "When I die, please have this passage read: 1 Thessalonians 4:13–18." We rushed to get the Bible and we read:

> But we would not have you ignorant, brethren, concerning those who are asleep, that you may not grieve as others do who have no hope. For since we believe that Jesus died and rose again, even so, through Jesus, God will bring with him those who have fallen asleep. For this we declare to you by the word of the Lord, that we who are alive, who are left until the coming of the Lord, shall not precede those who have fallen asleep; For the Lord himself will descend from heaven with a cry of command, with the archangel's call, and with the sound of the trumpet of God. And the dead in Christ shall rise first; then we who are alive, who are left, shall be caught up together with them in the clouds to meet the Lord in the air; and so shall we always be with the Lord. Therefore comfort one another with these words. (RSV)

We looked at each other and whispered in amazement, "An angel!"

Mother, unable to write or speak for that last year, still knew how much we loved her, how we believed in her healing . . . and how devastated we would be by her death. The Lord also knew all this. He, who had created Mother, knew the number of her days. And so he sent the perfect message from his word to reassure us that someday we would all be together again. His unfailing love sustained and comforted us as we buried Mother.

Three weeks after Mother died, my dad telephoned me. His voice was tight with emotion. "Oh, Susie," he whispered, "if only I could have the faith of a child again. I've grown up and, Lord, I'm so sorry."

I didn't know any words that could possibly console my dad that cold, dark, winter night. I listened as he continued to tell me that "Life has taught me how to fear and worry. I need to trust God more."

"You do trust him, Daddy," I replied. "Your words tonight are very precious. I hear something more in them. I believe God has given us a song."

The next afternoon I wrote a poem from the words that my father had expressed out of his sorrow. As I wrote, I could hear music. I had never "heard" music before. I went downstairs and tapped out the melody on the piano, writing the letters for the notes above the words of the poem. I phoned Dad and sang our song to him.

"That's it!" he told me. "That's it exactly."

God gave us that song to remind us of His unfailing love. He had also sent a heavenly messenger to comfort our grieving family. And still, I could not understand why I had believed Mother would be healed on earth, why my faith was so strong and yet she died.

One morning I was awakened before dawn by a loud voice. "What if you hadn't believed?" the voice boomed. Startled, I opened my eyes and sat up in bed. Moments later, it gently asked, "And who gave you your faith?"

I bowed my head, truly amazed and humbled by God's love reaching down to me. If I hadn't believed he would heal her, I would have always felt it was perhaps my "lack of faith" which kept Mother from being healed. If I hadn't seen beyond those dreadful circumstances, I could never have told Mother of the joy that overflowed from my heart.

It was then I remembered three special things Mother had said after her diagnosis. Upon receiving the diagnosis, in her hospital bed, looking small and wistful, she told us: "I only know that whatever time I have left here on earth, I want to use it to serve God. That is my prayer."

After she was pronounced healed, the first words she shared wherever she was invited to speak were: "Job said, 'the thing I fear the most will come upon me.' The thing that I feared the most was cancer. It 'came upon me.' But God is greater than cancer and he healed me."

And Mother confessed to us: "I know I have committed many sins. I have tried to be good and do what pleases God. But one sin that concerns me so is that perhaps I have loved my family more than God."

I never thought much about her saying that at the time. She loved the Lord so very much. Her faith had always been an important part of her life. And I knew we were very precious to her, too.

The night before Mother died, my sister and I sat on either side of her bed and softly sang her favorite hymns to her. We read her Bible to her. We marveled that the passages she underlined in her Bible were also the ones we had treasured and underlined in ours.

It seemed that the Lord allowed us each to minister to the other. Mother, though mute and "unresponsive" that last year of her life, was, indeed, still ministering to us. She served God the first years after her healing by going into her community, telling her story, and encouraging others. But the Lord, knowing each of our needs, also allowed her to continue serving him by ministering to those she loved so very much . . . her family.

I believe that just as the Lord used Mother's body to give me physical birth, He used her illness and death to accomplish my spiritual rebirth, and that of our family too. She had three years, from the time the doctors made their diagnosis, to touch many lives, to share her faith with others. I am in awe when I think of the way the Lord answered Mother's prayer. I am so grateful for the song he gave to my father and me. And I am continually amazed by his unfailing love.

Faith is the daring of the soul to go farther than it can see.
—WILLIAM NEWTON CLARK

GOD DOESN'T LET YOU GO

TERRY L. PAULSON, PH.D.

"I once visited a theological seminary and, for a long time afterward, I struggled to recover my sense of joy." —Norman Vincent Peale

Those unsettling words from Norman Vincent Peale ring true in describing the darkest days in my walk with God. For many believers called to serve, their time at seminary is a time of nurturing and an opportunity for deepening their faith. In some ways for me it was that, but, as I studied both the precepts of my faith and the principles of my emerging profession as a psychologist, my faith took a back seat to my struggle to understand and control God.

Even though I searched and studied diligently for understanding, I expected that surely at a seminary God would give me a deeper faith and growth in grace. Instead, the joy and the simple faith that had served me as a young man gave way to intellectual one-upmanship. Assertive psychologists trying to make their mission and message relevant and threatened theology faculty trying to solidify their place of power in the seminary hierarchy played volleyball with my mind. I left seminary six years later with every degree I had pursued, but with a deep disillusionment and a faith in hibernation.

Not all of our spiritual struggles as Christians require bouncing back from external tragedies or crippling losses. Sometimes one's most difficult challenges come from within. In the ensuing years I would come to learn a very important lesson: as we journey through the valley of the shadow of life in the fast lane, even when we think we are doing fine alone, God does not forsake his sheep.

I sublimated my disillusionment and spiritual conflict by reaching out for the "good life" or, as we used to say, "going for the gusto." The specifics of my fall would be hard to see for those watching on the sidelines of my life. On the surface, things went well. Already used to poverty in school, it was the best time to start my own company. After all, I had little to lose and a dream I believed I could achieve. Riding the hot topic of assertiveness, our company and profits grew. The balance sheet took a turn to the positive as my counseling clients gave way to speaking to associations and corporations throughout the country. I had made a name for myself, and I had made it without God—or so I thought.

Yet something was missing. I would certainly not have admitted it to anyone, much less myself. While I played the game of life as I knew it, God walked silently beside me, patiently waiting for me to return to the fold.

Even on the sidelines, evidence of problems were beginning to show. There was a divorce that shocked my family and friends. As I tried to pull my life back together, going to church was not part of the answer. I was a psychologist and an assertive one at that. I was sure that I could take care of my own life without any help from man or God.

I stayed busy as a full-time speaker and trainer, a part-time dad, and a budding partner to my new wife-to-be. The money was tighter, but I was happier. I knew I could be successful, and it wasn't too many years before my accountant confirmed that it was true. I had made it. In my mind there was no need for God.

But the Good Shepherd knows his sheep, and for that one lost sheep he would wait. . . .

Soon we were in our new home and my speaking career was blossoming. My accomplishments were even beginning to match what I said in my brochures!

On one trip, after speaking to a three-thousand-person audience in Minneapolis, I called home between planes. My wife had a little surprise.

"I hope you're sitting down," Lorie said with a smile in her voice. "I got a little surprise dropped off today. Your son is here to live with us."

Yes, my ten-year-old son, whom we had seen regularly on weekends and for more extended times on vacations, was doing more than just visiting. He had decided to live with us.

I have only respect for my ex-wife's wisdom in letting him make that choice; it could not have been easy for her to do. For Lorie and me there were moments of joy, concerns, new plans, and many new responsibilities. No more part-time parents; he was here for the long haul. God's lost sheep had all of a sudden taken on a herd.

In fact, little did I know that it was through Sean that God would reach out to touch both myself and my wife.

Like many Americans caught up in the good life, for us Sunday church just never seemed important enough to attend. Maybe if they had made every day Easter we might have made a point of attending. For Lorie and me, Sunday was a day we could sleep in, go for a long run, or do a 10K race.

But Sean changed all that. We now had an emerging teenager on our hands. How did we cope? We did what every panicked new parent does—we did what our parents did! We decided to take him to church to get a good grounding. To us, whether God joined us there was not essential; we would settle for the good grounding.

The Good Shepherd was opening a gate to the pasture he had been preparing for us.

There were churches visited, but not felt. There were weekends when our Sunday road race made attending any church out of the question. After all, it was a good-looking T-shirt, and what we were doing was for our health.

But one Sunday, with no race to run, we found our way to Westlake Lutheran Church. We felt the smiles, the outstretched hands, and the warm appeal of a minister who obviously cared. There is that great gospel song, "You're the Only Jesus Some Will Ever See." How true it was for us that day! Jesus came to us through Eileen Green, Mary Ann Fiore, even Pastor Lawson himself.

Jesus touched us anew that Sunday. Sean wanted to go back and so did we.

Deep faith eliminates fear.
—LECH WALESA

VICTORY OVER FEAR

ALEXANDER PLUMMER

rom out by the pool I could hear the phone ring. I was clearing sycamore leaves off the top of the water and emptying out the filter. The jasmine was fragrant and the oranges were just ripening. Off in the distance the mountains shimmered in the clear blue morning sky. "Alexander," I told myself, "you are truly blessed." The Lord had given me a wonderful wife, a fine house and a successful security business that I was soon to retire from. I had a positive attitude about life.

"It's for you," Beverly called from the house. I wiped my hands and went into the kitchen. "It's the doctor," she said. "He needs to speak with you."

A wave of anxiety broke over me, like a dam had burst somewhere inside. Normally I'm not afraid of anything. I'd never been sick in all my sixty-five years—never even missed a day of work. Good health was another one of my blessings. But then a routine blood test at my annual physical showed I had a high level of something called PSA, or prostate-specific antigen. Beverly, a nurse, had told me it could indicate a problem and insisted I get a biopsy.

"Mr. Plummer," the doctor said, "the biopsy has come back positive. It means you have prostate cancer. I'd like you to come in so we can discuss treatment."

I sank down into a chair at the kitchen table and stared at the telephone in my hand. "What's wrong?" Beverly said. I handed the phone back to her. She had to make the appointment for me.

Prostate cancer. My dad had died of prostate cancer when he wasn't much older than me. A hard-working Carolina sharecropper, he'd never been sick a day in his life either. Then one day he felt a pain in his side. He went to the doctor—the first time ever. They took him to the hospital and opened him up, then they closed him right back up. There was nothing they could do. *I'm going to die just like Dad did.*

"Alex," Beverly finally asked, "aren't you going to the gym today?" I went to the gym every morning.

I shook my head. Not today. I went back out by the pool. Was it only minutes earlier that I had been so happy with the good life God had brought me? The buddies I had, the trips Beverly and I went on, our children and grandchildren. Now God was going to take it away from me. My dad, two uncles, and several cousins had died of the same disease. Was this a family curse?

At breakfast the next morning I sat pushing my spoon around in my cereal. And I was a guy who loved to eat. At dinner I didn't come close to cleaning my plate. That night I lay around watching TV. The Kings were playing, but I couldn't keep my mind on the game. I kept thinking about my dad, about prostate cancer draining the life out of him in just two months. I had it too. I could almost sense it draining my life, and I was helpless to fight back. I'd never felt so vulnerable to something so beyond my control.

"Alex, honey." Beverly stood between me and the TV to get my attention. "This isn't like you. Stay positive. Wait until you hear what the doctor has to say about your treatment."

"Okay," I said, but I couldn't stop myself from feeling the way I did. Not when I'd been given a virtual death sentence. Beverly went up to bed. I stayed in the den, staring at the TV. If I didn't fall asleep, maybe I wouldn't wake up dead.

My visit to the doctor's office only made things worse. "What are you here for?" I asked one of the guys in the waiting room. "I had surgery for prostate cancer," he said. "Now I feel like a baby. Can't even control my own bladder." Others nodded. I picked up a brochure, but had to stop at the fine print about how a man could lose his sexual function. I barely heard a word the doctor said during our discussion about treatment.

"I'm not going to let anybody cut me up," I told Beverly later.

"Alex, there are other treatments. Get a second opinion. Look at the options." She would have dragged me all over town, but I wouldn't go. Why, when I'd just be told more that I didn't want to hear?

Still weighing my options, I closed down my business, Plummer Security, said goodbye to my clients like I was heading for my own funeral. Wouldn't let anyone give me a retirement party. Normally I loved being around the guys, joking and telling stories. Now their company just reminded me how happy I used to be, how much I'd be missing out on once cancer got me.

At the gas station one day I ran into one of my friends from the gym. "Alex," he said, "where have you been, buddy? If you don't get back on that treadmill, you'll put on twenty pounds."

"I'm not up to it anymore." Truth was, I'd lost about twenty pounds.

"You could come by and say hello."

"Sure," I said, knowing I wouldn't. About my only exercise was cleaning the pool. Sunday mornings, instead of heading to church, I'd turn on the TV to one of those preachers telling you how God loved you and wanted to save you. Sure, I thought. Then why is he letting the good life he's given me end just like that?

I tried to get my positive attitude back. I tried to tell myself medicine had come a long way since my dad's time. But no matter how hard I tried, I always slipped back into that fearful sense of despair I woke up to and went to sleep with every day and night. My daughter Cheryl called me daily and my brother Miller phoned long-distance from New York. He was a deacon in his church and full of faith. "Brother, you used to be closer to God than I was," he said one day. "You didn't worry about a thing. You trusted the Lord completely."

"That was before I had cancer."

"Now's the time you need God most. He's ready to help. Close your eyes and pray with me on the phone right now. 'Lord, cure my brother, Alex, of all his fears. Be with him in his suffering. . . . '"

No way could I find the energy to pray. My head was too filled with worries.

Finally Beverly sat me down. "Prostate cancer isn't the only disease you've got. You're not eating. You mope around all day. You lie in front of the TV and don't sleep at night. You're clinically depressed. You've got to get help, Alex."

I knew she was right, but I couldn't believe anyone could help me. After our talk, though, I prayed for the fear and depression to be lifted. I'm not sure I believed it would help, but I knew of no other option. *Lord, show me a way out.*

One Sunday a couple months after that morning I got the phone call from my doctor, I saw a 60 Minutes segment about a new treatment for cancer called proton-beam radiation. No surgery was involved, and there were few side effects. It was especially effective for prostate cancer. There was a place right here in Southern California that was using it, Loma Linda University Medical Center.

For an instant I felt those negative feelings well up as if to snatch this one ray of hope from me. *No,* I said to myself, *you've got to try.* "Beverly," I announced, "I'm going to get treated at Loma Linda."

My insurance plan rejected the expensive proton-beam treatments, so I changed coverage, which took months. The longer I waited, the more I struggled with depression. Now, at least, I was trying to fight back. Worries assaulted me. When the treatments finally started, I'd lie there terrified. I kept thinking of Dad and how his trip to the doctor was the beginning of the end.

I finally unloaded to the doctor at Loma Linda. "Your wife is right," he said. "Your fears have broken you down to the point that you are clinically depressed. That's only natural with a life-threatening disease. But you can't keep all those negative feelings inside. Talk to people. Talk to us. A good positive attitude is absolutely crucial when someone is facing cancer. It's the first step in treatment and the best way you can help yourself."

A positive attitude is the best way to help yourself. And what had always kept me so positive through my life? The answer was simple. My brother had seen it. I trusted that the Lord would bless me no matter what happened.

After the treatments I had to wait six months before the doctor could test my PSA to see if they'd worked. I'd never waited for anything so hard in my life.

"Man, I don't know how long I can take this," I told Miller on the phone. "The treatments were okay, but the suspense about them working is killing me."

"Don't give in to fear," Miller said. "You've got to trust God."

"When the worries take over, I sometimes forget that God is around."

"Then let him take the worry. Give it all to him, Alex."

I went outside and sat by the pool. "Lord," I said, "I've had enough of worrying. Your turn. You take it on. I don't want to be afraid anymore."

I heard the breeze ripple across the water and felt a load lifting from me. In flooded enormous gratitude for everything people had done for me. Miller's prayers, Cheryl's thoughtful phone calls, the support from our other kids, Beverly's patience, all of the help the staff at Loma Linda had given me. My true blessings in life weren't so much the things God had given me, but the very fact that he was always near.

Something changed after that. Not that the old energy came back immediately, or my appetite. What mattered was I finally realized I wasn't alone. Never had been. Watching TV in my lounge chair or sitting in the Jacuzzi, I knew people were fighting for me, and God was looking out for me above all.

I took a part-time job at Costco and started going back to the gym. The guys in line for the treadmill welcomed me like some kind of hero.

Finally I had the long-awaited blood test. I was as edgy as a coyote as Beverly and I waited for the results.

The doctor opened his folder and looked at the chart. "Good news, Mr. Plummer. Your PSA is down to zero-point-eight, well within the safe range."

I looked over at Beverly and began to laugh. She started laughing too. We jumped up and hugged each other, and when we got outside, I practically ran the two blocks to the car. I could have run a marathon. I felt that good.

Since then my PSA has gone down even more, and my depression has lifted completely. My old positive attitude is back. To keep it, I've got to share it. That's why I spend time at churches speaking to men about prostate cancer—especially black men, like me, who are statistically more at risk. I tell them it's natural to feel afraid, to feel more down than you've ever felt. I explain about the different treatments and that knowledge can combat fear. And there is faith to keep you going when those fears get the best of you. I tell them what I learned. When you have so much worry that you close off everybody, that's the time to give your worries to God. As Miller would say, God can take 'em.

AUTHOR INDEX

TITLE INDEX

Acknowledgments (continued from page 4)
Duffy, Karen. "Model Patient" from *Model Patient*. Copyright © 2000 by Karen Duffy, Cliff Street imprint of HarperCollins. Used by permission of HarperCollins. Epstein, Fred. "Brought Down to Ground Level" and "Only Crabs Go Backwards" from *If I Get To Five* by Fred Epstein and Joshua Horwitz. Copyright © 2003 by the authors. Published by Henry Holt and Co. Gill, Katie. "Nintendo Master" from *Chicken Soup for the Surviving Soul,* published by Health Communications, Inc. Reprinted by permission of Kathleen A. Gill. Inouye, Daniel K. "Pearl Harbor" from *Journey To Washington.* Copyright © 1967 by Prentice-Hall, Inc; Copyright renewed © 1995 by Daniel K. Inouye. Reprinted by permission of Simon & Schuster Adult Publishing Group. Joyner-Kersee, Jackie. "The Lesson" from *A Kind of Grace,* written with Sonja Steptoe. Copyright © 1997 by Jackie Joyner-Kersee. Used by permission of Warner Books, Inc. McCain, John. "Keeping Faith" from *Faith of My Fathers* by John McCain and Mark Salter. Copyright © 1999 by the authors. Used by permission of Random House, Inc. Meili, Trisha. "I'm Okay" from *I Am the Central Park Jogger: A Story of Hope and Possibility.* Copyright © 2003 by Trisha E. Meili. Used by permission of Scribner, an imprint of Simon & Schuster Adult Publishing Group. Nielsen, Jerri, Dr. An excerpt from *Ice Bound* by Dr. Jerri Nielsen with Maryanne Vollers. Copyright © 2001 by Dr. Jerri Nielsen. Reprinted by permission of Hyperion/Miramax. Parks, Rosa. "The Front of the Bus" from *Rosa Parks: My Story* by Rosa Parks with Jim Haskins. Copyright © 1992 by Rosa Parks. Used by permission of Dial Books for Young Readers, a division of Penguin Young Readers Group, Penguin Group (USA) Inc. Paulson, Terry L., Ph.D. "Real Strength" from *Whatever Happens, You Too Can Bounce Back,* compiled by Diana L. James, Horizon Books. Used by permission of the author. Pendergast, Chris. "Real Strength" from *Teachers With the Courage to Give,* edited by Jackie Waldman. Used by permission of Conari Press, an imprint of Red Wheel/Weiser. Reeve, Christopher. "Facing My New Life" from *Still Me* by Christopher Reeve. Copyright © 1998 by Cambria Productions, Inc. Used by permission of Random House, Inc. Scott, Mary Alice. "Doing Small Things With Great Love" from *Stories of the Courage to Teach,* compiled by Sam M. Intrator. Used by permission of John Wiley & Sons, Inc. Thomas, Dave. "Stands Are Good, Steps Are Better" from *Well Done* by Dave Thomas with Ron Beyma. Copyright ©1994 by R. David Thomas. Used by permission of The Zondervan Corporation. Warren, Andrea. "Missing Ben" from *Ladies Home Journal,* December 1997. Used by permission of the author. West, Marion Bond. "One Simple Word From God." Used by permission of the author.

All other selections originally appeared in *Guideposts* magazine or *Angels on Earth* magazine or were submitted to Guideposts for publication, and appear here for the first time. These selections are under copyright © by Guideposts, Carmel, NY.

Every effort has been to acknowledge the copyright and ownership of each selection. If any errors have occurred, correction will be made in subsequent editions, upon notification to the publisher.